Yesterday in Oshkosh
...my Hometown

By
Randy R. Domer

© 2012 Randy R. Domer
All Rights Reserved.

No part of this publication may be reproduced, stored in a retrieval system, or transmitted, in any form or by any means, electronic, mechanical, photocopying, recording, or otherwise, without the written permission of the author.

First published by Dog Ear Publishing
4010 W. 86th Street, Ste H
Indianapolis, IN 46268
www.dogearpublishing.net

dog ear PUBLISHING

ISBN: 978-1-4575-1588-0

This book is printed on acid-free paper.

Printed in the United States of America

*Dedicated to my family, friends
and people that touched my life along the way...*

Table of Contents

Preface v
Introduction 1
Drive Ins 9
Grocery Stores 25
Mark Gruenwald 34
Home Delivery 38
The Athearn 42
The Legion on the Lake 54
Knaggs Ferry 60
Richard Reichenberger 65
Trail's End 69
Sawyer Street Ball Diamond 72
Sports Heroes 74
Robert Lautenschlager 92
Children's Day Parade 98
Downtown 101
Television and Radio 107
Ralph Ott 111
Theaters 118
Telephones 134
Garlic Island 136
Winnebago County Airport 146
Pizza Parlors 150
Ice Skating 157
Readin', Ritin' and Rithmetic 159
Service Stations 167
The Fairgrounds 170
November 22, 1963 177
Credits 179
About the Author 180

PREFACE

"Where you from?"

"Oshkosh," I beamed. "Oshkosh, Wisconsin! It's between Green Bay and Milwaukee." Usually the reply was "Oshkosh B'Gosh!" or "The Airshow…Yeah, we've been there!" Well, of course you have. Everybody knows about Oshkosh. Or so it seemed to me.

I feel fortunate to have been born and raised here. But I don't think I truly realized why until I reached adulthood. Like many folks, as my career interests developed and changed, the need to move from my hometown was inevitable. My family thought I was crazy. "Move away from Oshkosh!?" You just didn't do that. My mother and aunt cried, my brother in law referred to us as "Gypsies" and we were scared to death. We were leaving the sanctity of familiar and safe surroundings. This was home.

But the separation caused me to see things differently. After a year of living out of state, it was on a return visit home that I realized something. People here spoke with an accent! I would go to the bank in my "new town" and people would ask, "Where you from?" "Oshkosh… Oshkosh Wisconsin!" I would proudly answer. "I thought so. It was either that or Minnesota, or something" they would mutter. As I drove through Milwaukee, heading north one weekend, I turned on the radio. "Listen" I said to Karen. "They really do have an accent here!" My wife Karen and I were both born and raised Oshkosh natives for 35 years and agreed it was funny we had never heard it before.

Moving away from Oshkosh helped us realize things that perhaps we previously took for granted. We missed our friends and family and the small hometown aura we felt when we returned back home. It was

Leon's frozen custard, or a terrific dinner at the Roxy… and how delicious are those Trail's End hot dogs! It's hard to make a stop at Fleet Farm and not run into a half dozen people you know. Our three daughters were born here, and both our parents and grandparents have passed away and are buried here. All our brothers and sisters still live here. This is our home. It always will be.

Recently, we retired, sold our home in Minnesota and returned home to Oshkosh. We live in a comfortable home on Lake Winnebago that welcomes us back to the place we grew up and have so many fond memories. You see, you can leave, but the need to keep some ties here are still strong.

The inspiration to write a book about growing up in Oshkosh came two summers ago.

My friend, Jim Senderhauf, likes to come over in the summer for morning coffee. Coincidently, he is married to my cousin, Dianne Ziebell Senderhauf. Jim faithfully brings a box of fresh doughnuts from Festival Foods and I supply the coffee.

Many mornings, we would sit on the porch and discuss local news and events. I was usually eager to hear from Jim because he was usually in tune with what was going on in town. I was always amused and interested in the countless stories Jim had to tell. Being about nine years my senior, Jim's background was a little deeper than mine. Jim has a great memory and can recall the names of each and every teacher he had from Kindergarten through high school. He even remembers telephone numbers and addresses from 50 years ago!

It is from those weekend morning coffee klatches I became inspired to try to recapture those earlier times…*the good old days*!

Also, I would like to acknowledge those that have gone before me to carve out priceless memories and capture important historical facts. Inky Jungwirth, Ed Tiedje, Ron LaPoint and others have written some excellent historical accounts and helped light the fires for me to do this.

Many books have been written about Oshkosh in the 1800's and early 1900's, but I hope to capture life here the way I remember it from my own childhood. It is my intent to recall things not as a historian, but as I remember them. I will rely on both personal experiences and also interviews with long time residents, friends and family to tell the story.

Preface

This undertaking has led me into research and historical fact finding that has been interesting and rewarding on so many levels. The personal interviews of people who lived here during the decades that precede me will help capture a snapshot in time with memories of life's experiences that someday will evaporate and be lost forever.

I will cover many topics and subjects along the way. Can you remember going to the outdoor theater? Driving past the "Rocket Corner" on the way to Sunlite's for an ice cream cone? Going to the theater on Saturday for the matinee? Or perhaps you can remember telephones before they had buttons or dials. I hope this book rekindles a few great memories for you, as it did for me.

Introduction

It was a different time. Life seemed so simple then.

Growing up on the west-side of Oshkosh was a little like living in the wilderness. Or so it seemed to me at the time. It was the 1950's when my parents decided to build a new home on North Lark Street. The only problem at the time was, no street system existed yet in that part of town, just vast, open fields and farmland. My dad purchased our property in the middle of the open field from my Uncle Neil Ziebell. He owned the tract of land that today basically encompasses Lark and Meadow Streets between Witzel and Southland Avenues. My mother's eldest sister, Aunt Loretta Ziebell, named Meadow Street as it was one block west of Lark Street and seemed appropriate. The bird names apparently caught on as other nearby streets were built (Hawk, Dove and Eagle).

The cross streets nearest our house on Lark were Witzel and Porter Avenues. Our mailbox was located on the corner of Lark St. and Porter Ave. It rested on top of an old wagon wheel, along with about eight other mailboxes. The wheel was mounted on a sturdy wood post that listed slightly to one side. We had to walk two blocks to get our mail along the dirt and gravel road between Witzel and Porter. It wasn't very long before other homes were built nearby, and the once remote wilderness started to take the shape of a neighborhood. North Lark Street then ran from Witzel Ave all the way to Sawyer Creek.

Because of where we lived, we were known as "West Siders". People in Oshkosh were categorized by where you lived. Other books written about Oshkosh by Inky Jungwirth and Ron Lapoint, identify the Hi-Holders from the south side and Nordheim to the north. The East-Siders or "fish eaters" lived basically east of Main Street to North Park (known as Menominee Park today). Ethnic groups seemed to migrate together. Germans, Polish and Russians were the predominant immigrant groups. Religious backgrounds were also very important. Catholic and Lutheran families did not approve of the other "marrying into the family" and there were times where families were irretrievably broken by "mixed marriages" of religion.

One of my earliest friends was Timmy Danner. The John and Carmen Danner family rented a farmhouse on the property near what today is North Eagle Street near Southland Avenue, across from what would become the location of Oshkosh West High School. Southland Ave did not exist then and Eagle Street was nothing more than a dirt road that lead from the Danner's north to where Pollock Pool is today. The Danner house provided some great space for young boys to explore and we found many exciting things to do. Abandoned buildings, sheds, corn cribs and a chicken coop was our playground. Where Eagle Street is today was the Danner yard, beyond that open farmland and fields stretched westward all the way to the current US Highway 41. The Danner yard and this farmland were separated by a single strand of barbed wire which we had no problem clambering over and under whenever we wanted. A couple of long forgotten apple trees provided some great climbing challenges and some pretty tasty apples as I recall. We even ate them green with a shaker of salt we secretly borrowed from Mom's cupboard. Mom always warned us that we would get a stomach ache, but we never let that stop us. When my Dad came home from work, it was time for supper. He would step out the back door, put two fingers in his mouth, and give out a whistle that I'm sure could be heard for a mile. That was my signal to come home. And boy, you didn't want to make him do it twice! My dad was a truck driver and worked for Steffke Freight which was located along the river where the University is today. In addition to his day job, he had a talent for drawing and painting. He "moonlighted" by lettering delivery vans for every pizza parlor in town. Jess and Nicks, Red's and West End were the big ones then. He also was friends with local stock car driver Dave Conger. Dad painted the old number 20 and added his version of Woody Woodpecker which became Conger's trademark.

Down the road from Danner's, where Pollock Pool sits today, was "The Woods". The Woods was undeveloped land and embraced Sawyer

INTRODUCTION

Creek as it wound its way toward the Fox River behind Pluswood, eastward through the woods and fields, narrowing as it passed beneath Highway 41. My buddies and I fished, caught frogs, picked wild strawberries and choke cherries and played hide and seek. As we got a little older, we would take our BB guns and take aim at,... well let's just say things that most of us probably wouldn't find acceptable today.

As kids, raiding gardens was one of our favorite pastimes. Considered harmless mischief in our day, at least by our standard, we would sneak into the neighbor's garden, and pick a few tomatoes or whatever we could find. Not that we were hungry or needed the produce, I just think it was the excitement of getting caught. That parcel of land where Oshkosh West High School sits today, hosted some of the most delicious peas you ever tasted. And sweet corn! We would fill up a paper sack with peas, sit in the back yard, and eat them all.

The oldest of three children meant having to look after my younger sister, Debbie, and little brother Corey. Many evenings were spent with the neighborhood gang playing "Kick the Can". Some evenings, like school nights, the rule was we could play outside until the streetlights came on. When I went to bed, I would fall asleep listening to the 18-wheelers travel down Highway 41. There were no houses in the way to block the sound. And no air conditioning meant the windows were always open, especially on those hot, sultry, summer evenings.

The Milwaukee Braves was my team. I would lay on my bed and listen to the radio broadcast on many evenings. I recall Blaine Walsh and Earl Gillespie calling the action over my radio for the Braves. I would spread my baseball card collection out on the bed and try to match the lineup for each game. Eddie Mathews and Hank Aaron were the one-two punch for the Tribe. The supporting cast included Joe Adcock, Roy McMillan, Frank Bolling and golden arms of Warren Spahn and Lew Burdette. Sometimes, my parents would let me lay in their bedroom and listen to the radio there. I could look out the front bedroom window and see the lights of the Sawyer Street ballpark glowing only 2 blocks away. I dreamed of what it would be like to be a major league ball player.

The neighborhood had several open fields for us to play ball in. Home plate was a 12 inch piece of a two-by-four. First base was a small piece of plywood and so forth. Needless to say, it made sliding a little precarious. One of our neighbors, Ray Smith, always had time after work to play ball with the neighborhood kids. He would pitch our taped up, worn out "league ball" underhand fashion and we would all take turns batting. Our bat was one we recovered from one of the Oshkosh Giant games at the Sawyer Street Ball Field. It was a broken bat, but we took it home, screwed it back together, and with the help of some of my dad's electrical tape, we were back in business.

As a boy, baseball was my passion. My interest in baseball was fueled by five-cent packs of cards sold at the check stand down at the Super Valu store on Sawyer Street. At ten years old, I managed to find some change now and then, at least enough to buy a pack or two of Topps finest. I would finger through the packs on display, trying to pick that lucky one that might have one of my favorite players. I ripped open each pack slowly, popped the piece of stale, tasteless gum into my mouth, and rifled through the players looking for that special one. Any of the Milwaukee Braves would be super, of course, but if it was Hammerin' Hank Aaron, I'd hit the jackpot! Having no idea those cards would someday increase in value; I kept them stashed under my bed, held by a rubber band in a cardboard box. Usually, they were sorted by teams, not card number. That way, when I listened to the Braves game on the radio, I could get the opposing team out, and lay the starting lineup out across the bed. I also did the unforgiveable. We would take a card and using a clothespin, attach it to the wheel of our bike, inserting the card through the spokes so when you rode it made a flapping sound. How cool was that? I wonder how many Mays and Mantles I destroyed doing that? I still have those 1961 cards today, and an accumulation of thousands of others.

After Christmas, the fields and empty lots in the neighborhood became the ideal locations to build a Christmas tree fort. As soon as the trees hit the curb, we grabbed them and dragged them to one of the empty field lots to create our fortress of evergreens. Artificial trees were rare at that time, so live trees were plentiful.

The snow banks back then would tower over our heads, or at least they seemed mountainous to us. Those snowbanks made a great base for tunneling and burrowing snow caves. The snow caves we created were fun to crawl around in but also served a dual purpose. They were a place to escape and hide after we tossed snowballs at a passing car.

Introduction

My school was Roosevelt. *Rose-a-velt…not Roo-sa-velt.* Other than the "rural schools" just west of Oshkosh, it was really the only public school on the westside (for clarification, the NEW Franklin School was considered the south side by us west-siders), I attended there K-9. School was about 8 blocks from where we lived. Therefore my options were to walk, or when I got a little older, ride my bike. Occasionally, when the weather was bad, we would get a ride to school, usually from a neighbor. Our family only had one car which my Dad drove to work every day. In my Roosevelt years, I had many friends. My closest buddies were Fred Auclair, Garrett Galica, Bill Zimmerman and Mike Lichtenwald who all lived several blocks away so it was a bike ride to get to each other's house. Right in our neighborhood, Keith Boushele and Jeff Zillges were always up for a ball game, building a fort or going down to Sawyer Creek fishing.

In the early 60's, we would race toward home after school, stopping at Stangel's Super Valu on Sawyer Street along the way. The Green Bay Packers were coming off another championship season and Coca Cola had a promotion where each bottle cap contained a picture of one of the Packers inside each bottle cap. This was before pop machines used cans. Twelve ounce bottles of Coke products all had the promotion. Patrons would put ten cents into the vending machine; a bottle of pop would slide down the chute. You then took the bottle and removed the cap using the bottle opener located on the front of the machine. The cap would fall down into a slot that held them all until they were discarded when the machine was restocked. We devised a system to retrieve these caps with a magnet on a string. We dropped the magnet down the chute, and let it attract a few bottle caps, and then slowly pulled it back out, being careful to not lose any on the way. As several of the neighborhood kids quickly caught on to this, it was important to be the first one there after school. Those caps were later redeemed for a football.

Many of the public schools in Oshkosh flooded ice rinks each winter and provided warming houses for skaters. We had a huge ice rink at Roosevelt. I remember a couple of the custodians and a neighbor who took care of it and supervised the warming house. My wife Karen remembers doing the same thing at Merrill School. Karen was, and still is, a very good skater. She recalls that she would skate all night until her feet hurt or her parents flashed the porch lights to come home.

My first bike was a beautiful blue Schwinn. Mom and Dad bought it at Vern's Cycle Center, on Main Street near Cook and Brown. The day we picked it up, my Dad said, "Why don't you ride it home?" It was a couple of miles from home and I had to go over the Wisconsin Avenue Bridge, but I was anxious to try it out. My Dad followed me with his car as I made my way down Radford Road toward Wisconsin Avenue. The railroad tracks there crossed the road at an angle. My front tire became wedged into the track and down I went. More embarrassed than hurt, I picked myself up, checked out my new bike for any scratches or damage, and then resumed my journey. I made it home just fine but was always cautious crossing railroad tracks from then on.

When I was 15, my parents allowed me to buy a motorcycle. I was now working at the Super Valu Store on Sawyer Street, so I had my own money. I went over to Ohio Street where Slim Davis owned a Harley Davidson Dealership. I saw my motorcycle right away. It was the bike of my dreams; a real beauty...a candy apple red, Bridgestone Sport 90cc. Several of my friends already had motorcycles...Fred Auclair, Garrett Galica and Dean Koechell. I took the bike home and was convinced by my buddies it would sound better if you sawed off the baffle shorter in the muffler, so I did it...much to the dismay of my Dad. But it was my first form of transportation and took me around town wherever I wanted to go. A few bucks of gas would last all week!

Anxious to expand my interest in music, I began accordion lessons at age ten. My neighbor and school mate Angie Smith had similar aspirations, so we both joined Oswald's Academy of Music. Our lessons were on Monday nights and our parents would take turns driving us there. My mother and my Grandma Domer both loved it when I played. I dreamed of having my own polka band someday and be right up there with Ralph Becker, Sam Oswald, Dodo Ratchman and all the other famous wedding bands in town. My Grandma Domer would come to visit, and ask me to get my accordion out while she dialed up her friends at the local nursing home. Her request was always the same. "Randy...play Whispering Hope" she would say. Then she'd hold up the phone so her friends could hear. By the time I was done, they all were crying. I loved that accordion!

You see, back then, we made our own fun. No Playstation, X Boxes, video games, cable or satellite TV. The three Green Bay TV channels we could receive offered little in the way of entertainment, but

INTRODUCTION

never knowing any different, we were satisfied. There were no cell phones, texting, tweeting, emails or *Facebook*.

We made our own life's experiences and adventures…

It was a different time. Life seemed so simple then.

Drive-Ins

In the 1950's and 60's, drive-ins were very popular. But we didn't call them "drive-ins", they were commonly referred to as "root beer stands". And Oshkosh certainly had its share. As a child, we would take the occasional Sunday afternoon drive which almost always ended at a drive-in for an ice cream cone, root beer or float. Dozens of businesses sprang up with each offering something a little different. Some had car hops while others had counters inside. Some had both. Some had speakers you would drive up to, place your order and someone would bring your food out when ready.

Several of the most memorable were located on or near Murdock Ave which was the mother lode of drive-ins at that time. The Hutch, Leon's, and Sno Cap were all located within two blocks of each other. In the 1960's McDonalds made its entrance into Oshkosh and started changing the landscape for drive-ins across the USA. The Southside was the home of the Hi-Holder while further south was home to Ardy & Ed's and the E&E …just to name a few.

Ardy & Ed's

Conspicuously located on a triangle intersection on the south side of the city, where business Highway 45 meets Doty St, sits one of the remaining jewels from the drive-in era. Our Sunday afternoon family drive would usually include a stop at this root beer stand, giving Mom a break from making supper that night.

Opened in 1948 as Southside A&W, Ardy & Ed's helps locals cling to the times where teens and families would drive up to enjoy the best root beer float in town. Still in the same location today, Ardy & Ed's continues to thrive by offering patrons delicious Americana fare, from burgers, fries, cones, shakes and floats to perch, chicken and shrimp baskets and much, much more. Diners today enjoy watching their car hop roller skate gracefully between the pickup window and your car while your favorite 50's and 60's tunes recreate the "Blast from the Past!" The roller skates were introduced in 1983 after the owners decided to pave the gravel parking lot. A couple of the girls working there liked to skate and asked if they could add it.

Current co-owner, Steve Davis offered me some background and personal insights into this famous Oshkosh "hotspot": *Through the years, Ardy and Ed's has been featured in numerous local and national publications and TV broadcasts, including 2005's "Roker on the Road" and in 2004, "Top Five Food Innovations" on the Food Network. In 2003, they were chosen as the #4 location on Mazda's "Top – 10 Down List" of places in the USA to go in a convertible. Most recently, a German media company filmed an episode of their documentary "As the World Eats," airing in the summer of 2009.*

One of the original owners included Nate Rohr (who also owned a number of other root beer stands in the Fox Valley) and in 1953 it was purchased by Robert and Elizabeth "Ollie" Albrecht. In 1957, current co-owner Ardy Davis started working there. In 1960, the restaurant was sold to Ollie Albrecht's son, Edward Timm, (who was the husband of Ardy). In 1972, the drive-in was renamed Ardy & Ed's. Ed has since passed, but Ardy and her husband Steve Davis still own and operate the drive-in today.

Steve Davis adds: *Today, Ardy, Steve and the staff of Ardy and Ed's strive to continue serving our customers only the best food, "Famous" draft root beer, "Old Fashioned" serving fountains with the same personal, friendly service which their customers have enjoyed for more than 60 years!*

Ardy & Ed's is only open seasonally, from March through September.

Ardy and Ed's Circa 2009
Photo Credit Randy Domer

The Hutch

The year was 1954. A local English professor at UW-O decided he wasn't making the standard of living that he wanted as an educator to support his family, and was looking for ways to subsidize his income.

Turn the clock back to 1940. As a student in his junior year at the university in Oshkosh, Earl Hutchinson worked in a drive-in located on the corner of North Main and Murdock.

Fourteen years later, he was now teaching at this same university as a Professor of English. One day, he became aware the drive-in where he worked as a student, was for sale.

Dr. Earl Hutchinson and his wife Jane decided they would buy it.

I met with Jane Hutchinson in September 2008, right after her 90th birthday. Ironically, we arranged to meet at another former A&W restaurant on Jackson Drive. Over a cup of coffee and some eggs, I listened to Jane reminisce about their days in the drive-in business. "That restaurant was our life!" It was truly a family affair as Earl, Jane and all eight of their children worked there performing various duties including cooking, car hopping, mixing A&W Root Beer, waiting on the counter, doing dishes…they did it all. In a 1989 Oshkosh Northwestern interview, Earl mused, "Those kids would do any job. In fact, they did things we wouldn't ask hired help to do!"

The Hutch's location was unique within itself. Located virtually yards from Leon's and Sno Cap, each drive in found its niche. The Hutch served some of the best root beer in town (one of two A&W franchises in Oshkosh), delicious sandwiches, hamburgers, hot dogs, ice cream, root beer floats and those ever-so-famous Black Cows! Baby root beers were served complimentary in little glass mugs.

Car hops would come to your car, sometimes arriving before the car rolled to a stop. They'd place a ticket with a number under your windshield wiper. Then they took your order and ran trays of food from the window to your car in minutes. Patrons would be coached to "roll your window up or down a bit" so the serving tray would hang on your car's window just right. When you were done, or needed something, you flashed your headlights to summon a car hop.

The Hutch was located right across the street from the Fairgrounds and only a few blocks from some of Oshkosh's seamier bars that featured topless dancers. "We had a real cross section of people as customers," Jane remembers with a smile. Regulars included everyone, from policemen to clergy. "The Winnebago County Fair was the busiest time of year for us. Fair goers would flock to The Hutch after leaving the fair, and late at night, when the fairgrounds closed, we got all the carnival employees. They were a little different but all were very nice folks" Mrs. Hutchinson recalled. At bar time, some of the girl dancers from the nearby "Go-Go Bar" would come to The Hutch for a bite to eat. As she sat with her hands folded, looking off in the distance, Jane recalled, "I remember some of those girls being so young. I would serve them a hot meal, and then I'd go back in the kitchen and cry. I felt *so* sorry for them."

Daughter Kim (Price) recalled the day she faced an armed robbery. "A woman pointed a gun at me from her car and demanded money. I was terrified!" Kim said. "She instructed me to go to another register to get the money. As I walked past Dad, I whispered to him…*She has a gun*!" Earl ordered everyone to the floor, locked the doors and called the police. The woman escaped but without any cash.

In 1962, The Hutch became the first drive-in in Oshkosh to stay open all year round. It was that same year tragedy struck. On September 7, The

Drive-Ins

Hutch was destroyed by fire. The only two things that survived the fire were a cash register tray and a porcelain owl. The owl would soon become the trademark for The Hutch. Earl took the damaged owl home and saved it.

A 1962 fire all but destroys a dream
Photo Credits: Jane Hutchinson

By 1963, The Hutch was back in business. The burned owl was placed symbolically next to the fireplace, and a new owl was placed across from it. That's when the collection started. People heard the story of the owl that survived the fire, and would bring in owls from all over. Earl estimated he had collected over 300 owls through the years.

The drive-in was an A&W franchise until 1974. The Hutchinson's operated the drive-in until 1977 when they decided to sell it and retire. No longer operating as a drive-in, the business still thrives today as The Chalice.

Leon's

When it came to drive-ins, Murdock Avenue was the ultimate. On one end of the block, The Hutch held the anchor spot on the corner of Murdock and Main Street. The west end of the block was occupied by the Sno Cap drive in. Located right between the two was the best frozen custard you would find for miles! Leon's Frozen Custard grew their version of the drive in business with a niche of offering something the others did not...creamy, smooth frozen custard. Vanilla and chocolate were the only two flavors of custard available.

Like their neighbors, Leon's was located directly across the street from the Winnebago County Fairgrounds. Fair goers would flock here after the fair to enjoy a cone, sundae, a hot dog or one of their famous "*Joosburgers.*" Every Tuesday night in the summer was racing night at Leo's Speedway, located across the street in the fairgrounds. Local stock car enthusiasts would cheer on their favorite driver, then cruise to Leon's afterwards for a sandwich or treat before going home.

Through the years, Leon's gained fame and notoriety for their delicious custard. In 2004 while campaigning in Wisconsin, President George W. Bush stopped his campaign bus at Leon's and walked to the window and ordered a vanilla custard!

Today, Leon's Frozen Custard still serves up the best there is when it comes to frozen custard in the same location (121 W. Murdock) since they opened in 1947. Current owners (2008) Christine & Michael Schraa, still run the business the way it was run over 50 years ago. The menu remains virtually unchanged. Carhops continue to eagerly serve drive up customers decked out in their 50's era poodle skirts. If you want a true sense of what drive-ins from the 50's were like, then drive over to Leon's today.

DRIVE-INS

Photo Credit: Randy Domer

Leon's Circa 2009
Photo Credit: Randy Domer

Sno Cap

As previously mentioned, Murdock Ave was the center of drive-ins in the 1950's and 60's. Sno Cap was just yards from the intersection of Jackson and Murdock... located next door to Nolte's Standard station. What distinguished Sno Cap from the other drive-ins in town was the long canopy which stretched from the front door all the way to Murdock Street. Patrons could pull their cars into a spot under the canopy where carhops would serve you. That really was nice during rainy days! The menu was fairly extensive, offering cones, sundaes, floats and a wide variety of hot sandwiches.

Sno Cap Drive In
Photo Credit: Ed and August Tiedje

This Oshkosh favorite began doing business in 1950 at 103 N. Murdock; then with the address change in 1958, it then became 307 W. Murdock. Mr. Glen Huntington was the original owner and, according to the 1951 Oshkosh City Directory, lived in Stoddard, WI. Huntington eventually moved to Oshkosh in 1961 purchasing a home right behind the drive-in at 1729 Kentucky Ave. He owned Sno Cap until

1963 when the business and residence on Kentucky Ave were sold to Garnett W. Calkins.

Three years later in 1966, a kid named Mike Strycker was looking for a job. He walked into Sno Cap and asked to speak with the manager. Ron Frey was fresh out of college and was the person Calkins hired to manage the drive-in. Strycker applied for the job of carhop, and Frey decided to give the kid a chance.

It was this meeting of fate that brought Ron and Mike together. Both were hard working and ambitious.

Mike Strycker serves up a cone in 1973
Photo Credit: Mike Strycker

In June of 1970, Ron Frey and Mike Strycker became new business partners and bought the Sno Cap Drive-In.

"We were always looking for ways to grow the business" Mike Strycker told me. He then added "The main blue and white canopy came from the old Mars Drive-In on Sawyer Street".

Strycker said their hamburgers were the best around. "We ground our own ground beef right there in the kitchen. We used an ice cream scoop to measure the right amount and plop it on the grill. Then we'd take a spatula and flatten it into a patty while it was cooking." The burger was then served on a Semmel roll...it was delicious!

Mike's wife Mary was also involved in the family business, more so at A&W than Sno Cap. "I remember we hired those kids to work for us because they would work the hours we needed them. They were probably only a couple of years younger than Mike and I but because we were "*The Bosses*" they seemed like kids to us."

Mary reminded Mike "Remember the Mad Dog?" Mike smiled and proceeded to explain this unusual concoction. "The Mad Dog was a glass root beer mug with ice, orange soda on the bottom, slowly topped off with root beer, then garnished with two pickles!"

The carhops would come to the car as soon as it arrived, and put a number under your windshield wiper. They would then take your order, handwritten on a restaurant notepad, and clothespin it to a wire. With a flick of the wrist, the order went flying along the wire directly into the kitchen area as the carhop hollered "ORDER!"

So many people were regulars at Sno Cap, but one that stands out in Mike Strycker's mind is Father Thompson. "Father Thompson always drove in and ordered a pizza burger and a cherry Coke" Mike recalled. "I knew him from Lourdes as he was a priest there. One day, in 1968, I had a religious medallion on a chain, and being Catholic I wanted to have it blessed. Father Thompson had just pulled in and I asked one of the carhops to ask him if he would bless my medallion". Then Mike smiled and said "He told the carhop to ask me to hold it up where I was working inside so I did. He then crossed himself did the blessing from his car!"

Leon's was a short block away with an empty lot separating the two. "They were our biggest competition, at least with our staff" Mary mused. "We had fun with it. We would count the number of cars in their lot compared to ours, we tried to be open before they were and at closing time, our kids would wait until Leon's turned off their lights before going dark at Sno Cap".

In 1973, Frey and Strycker decided they wanted to get into the franchise restaurant business and were awarded an A&W franchise. The new restaurant was built on Jackson Ave, a short distance from their Sno Cap Drive-In and opened on September 26, 1973. Mike and Ron split their duties between Sno Cap and the A&W until 1980...then the partnership dissolved. "Ron is a great guy and we remained friends all along. We just had different ideas on the direction we wanted to go".

Frey kept the Sno Cap business while Strycker the A&W. In 1982, Frey took the big step to remodel Sno Cap into a restaurant with indoor seating and a very contemporary design. In 1984, Ron Frey left Sno Cap and moved to Arizona to pursue other interests. Sno Cap Drive-In was then acquired by Vitale's, who operates a restaurant today on that once vacant lot between Sno Cap and Leon's.

Mike and Mary Strycker owned the A&W and after the partnership with Frey ended, the decision was made to convert the drive-in to an indoor seating format. Mike talked about this transition. "We had already altered the A&W menu by adding items like hot beef sandwiches with mashed potatoes and a full breakfast menu. We really wanted to move from the drive-in format to the *coffee shop* model. It was then Stryckers decided to drop the A&W franchise and changed the name to *Mike's Place*. But this was no easy going according to Mike. "We had a 30 year contract with A&W. After several high level meetings with A&W Corporate, we were released from our contractual agreement."

In 2000, *Mike's Place* was sold to one of Stryckers employees…Seth Murphy.

Today, *Mike's Place* is still part of Mike Stryckers routine. He goes there every morning, 7 days a week as part of his morning ritual. He comes inside before the business is open and I'm told he is the only one allowed to do this. He greets the staff, walks over to the coffee pot he was so familiar with all those years, pours himself a cup and grabs the morning paper, waiting for the place to open. When it does, Mike is joined by a group of fellas he served morning coffee to for so many years. Mike looked at me proudly and said "It's what I do. I built that place… and it still means a lot to me"

Mars

Growing up on the west side meant we had few offerings for drive-ins or root beer stands we could reach by foot or by bicycle, which were our main means of transportation. In the 50's and 60's, our parents didn't jump at the drop of a hat to run us around to various locations or activities. You rode your bike, walked or took the bus.

My earliest memory of Mars was a small ice cream cone stand located on the southwest corner of Taft and N. Sawyer. (Before the city address change in 1957, the address was 217 N. Sawyer, then became 515 N. Sawyer). Erwin and Martha Kitzman (Martha is who Mars was named after) operated a small stand that had no seating and parking was mostly along the street.

Most of the business was for ice cream cone walkups. We would walk up to a window on the Sawyer Street side, where Mr. Kitzman would peer through the small window and take your order. When ready, he would slide the small screen to side and hand you your cone.

Eventually, the Kitzmans' son Dave became involved in the business and expanded the small building by adding a glass enclosure where patrons could get out of the weather to place their order to go. I remember them advertising a shake, a hamburger and fries for 15 cents each. This early version of today's "value meal" would cost 45 cents. Shakes came in three flavors, vanilla, chocolate and strawberry. Mars eventually expanded the menu to include Lake Perch buckets as a Friday special, and various other items as well. My favorite was the "Martian Burger", very similar to McDonalds "Big Mac". At Mars, the slogan was "Our food is out of this world!"

In the early 1960's a canopy was added to allow customers to drive up and park under shelter. By the late 1960's, the canopy and the original small building came down (the canopy was sold to cross town business rival Sno Cap) and the restaurant was rebuilt and expanded to include indoor seating and brick façade on the exterior. Mars quickly became the local "hangout" for "west-siders". It was there one evening during the summer of 1967 that my "wife-to-be" cruised through the parking lot with a friend. I ran out to say hi but she was gone…just like that. I went to the nearest pay phone located on the back wall of the dining area, looked her address up in the phone book, tore it out and coaxed my best friend, Fred Auclair, to drive me to her house on Tennessee Ave. The rest is history. Karen still has that torn phone book page tucked away in a memory box.

Mars opened in 1958 and changed ownership several times eventually becoming a corporation with over 20 stores. No Mars drive-ins exist today. Currently, the original location is the home of the family style Delta Restaurant and still serves great food.

Mars Drive-In 1964
Photo Credit: Dan Radig

The Hi-Holder

On the corner of Fifth and Knapp Streets, sat a quaint little drive-in. Aptly named "The Hi-Holder" in honor of the surrounding neighborhood, this drive in was a regular stop on our way to the 44 Outdoor on Friday and Saturday nights. My dad would buy a bag of burgers, mom would pack a cooler with some pop, and off we would go. We would arrive at the Outdoor a little early so we could eat before the movie started and it was still light outside.

According to the Oshkosh City Directory, the Hi-Holder began doing business in 1949. Records indicate that Robert W. Geffers was the sole owner of the business until it closed in 1967. After that, Geffers is still listed as the owner of the building as recently as 2002.

People who lived in the Sixth Ward, that is the area around the old Sacred Heart Church, between Witzel Ave and Ninth St., were considered *High Holders* as they were of Bohemian descent. A recent German immigrant once explained to me that the term *Hi-Holder* referred to people who worked in the fields gathering hay. As many families kept livestock, goats, sheep, etc. they needed hay for feed.

The Hi-Holder Drive-In
Photo Credit: Ed and August Tiedje

This part of the city was still urban and immigrants that settled here worked to create a "village –like" concept similar to their homeland. Most of the men were blue collar laborers who worked in the local mills and manufacturing plants in town. The Paine Lumber company was one of the largest employers. My wife Karen's grandfather, Joseph Sosnoski, lived on Seventh Avenue and worked at Paine Lumber.

The Hi-Holder was an eating place the locals could relate to. Good food at fair prices.

E&E

In the 1950's, it was not uncommon for drive-ins to be located close to one another as was the case on Murdock with Leon's, Sno Cap and The Hutch. On the opposite and far edge of town on South Main Street, the A&W (now Ardy and Ed's) and the E&E were directly across the street from one another, right across the street from Lake Winnebago. The E&E was a bit smaller of the two and famous for their nickel root beers and 21 Shrimp Basket.

E&E Drive-In
Photo Credit: August and Ed Tiedje, FB

According to the City Directory, the business was owned by Emil Repp from the mid 40's as a root beer stand, and later converted to a Produce stand. The building was razed in 1996.

The Blue Ox, The Airport Drive-In and Marty's Drive-In and more...

The Blue Ox Drive-In was located on Jackson Drive, three blocks north of the fairgrounds. Unique in its own right, Yidda Malchow owned and operated the only root beer stand in town where you could get a cold beer with your hot dog.

Harry's Drive-In was also on Jackson Drive, about 1 mile north of Murdock. Harry's offered both curbside and counter service and featured charcoal broiled food with everything from sandwiches to lobster and they were open daily from 6am to midnight.

Albert and Pauline Binder, owners of The Airport Drive-In, invited patrons to watch the planes landing and taking off while enjoying a malt and your favorite sandwich. Located at 805 W. 20th, between the intersections of Delaware and Georgia, it was just a short drive from Ardy and Ed's and the E&E toward the lake.

Marty's Drive-In sat near the corner of Ceape and Rosalia. Like several other drive-ins in town, Marty's offered both car service or inside seating.

Drive in TO HARRY'S CHARCOAL BROIL DRIVE-IN
1 Mile North on Jackson Street Road
● NOW ●
CURB-SERVICE AND COUNTER SERVICE
Featuring:
- FISH
- SHRIMP
- LOBSTER
- SCALLOPS
- SHORT ORDERS
- SANDWICHES, ALL KINDS
- HO-MADE SOUP AND PIES
- TAKE HOME ORDERS

Open 6 A.M. to Midnight

MARTY'S DRIVE-IN
Corner Ceape and Rosalia

Car Service As Well As Ample Seating Inside

— We Specialize In —
Take Out Orders
Phone Blk. 6036

- Chicken ● Shrimp
- Fish ● Steak Sandwiches
- Hamburger ● Hot Beef
- Bratwurst ● Bar-B-Ques
- Cheeseburgers ● Etc.

HI FOLKS! AIRPORT DRIVE-IN WILL OPEN SATURDAY, MAY 1st
Serving Those Delicious Malts and Sandwiches
Come and See Us on the 20th Street Road
Albert and Pauline Binder, Props.

Grocery Stores

If you were around in the 1950's or earlier, you probably remember the corner "Mom and Pop" grocery store. Every neighborhood had one. No matter where you lived, you didn't have to travel more than a few blocks to find one. Automobiles were a luxury back then and most families only owned one, if they had one at all. People relied largely on the bus, bicycles or walking for transportation when the family car was not available.

These "corner stores" were family owned and operated. Most offered mainly dry grocery goods because commercial refrigeration was not yet fully developed. Stand alone fresh meat markets offered custom cuts of fresh meat, sold over a full service meat case. Customers were waited on by a staff of butchers who knew their trade and knew it well. In those days, the butcher was one of the most trusted people a person did business with. You trusted him when you called up and ordered your meat, that he was going to "hand select" only the best cuts of beef, pork and chicken for you. By the 1950's, many corner grocery stores installed refrigeration, offering meat, produce and dairy and thus became the beginning of "one-stop shopping".

On the west side, my memories of neighborhood stores include Weigandt's and Hartman's on Sawyer St., Werner's on Oshkosh Ave., and Reichenbergers on Knapp. I was most familiar with Weigandt's and Hartman's as they were near Roosevelt School. I would stop by after school on occasion when my mother would give me some money. At Weigandt's, the front door led up some steps. On the left was a long glass enclosed case where the penny candy was sold. Mrs. Emma Weigandt would sit behind the counter and patiently wait for us to make that difficult choice on how we would spend that nickel or dime. At Hartman's, the store front had two separate doors. Customers entered the left door if they wanted groceries, the right door if they wanted fresh meat. Hartman's was one of a handful of neighborhood stores in town then that had custom cut meats. In the 1950's there were separate "butcher shops" that sold only meat. The two I remember best were Buehler Brothers on Main Street and Shubert's Meat Market on Oshkosh Avenue, at the end of Sawyer Street. My mom would take me in as she ordered her pork chops or roast for our Sunday dinner and often a ring of bologna for a week night meal. Smells of fresh smoked sausage filled the air. The long, glass front meat case was often fogged up and covered with condensation during the hot summer months. While my mom was deciding what she wanted, the butcher would reach into the case, break off a hot dog from the pile of linked wieners and hand it to me. That ended up being a tradition I carried on later in life when I cut meat.

Home delivery of groceries is not something new. I remember seeing Wally Rosanske from Werner's Market on Oshkosh Ave, walking down the street, sporting his clean, crisp white apron, en route to deliver a bag or two of groceries to a neighbor. Customers would often use credit and pay at the first of the month, or when they could. Sometimes, if things were difficult, especially during the hard times, they couldn't pay at all.

Wally Rosanske sweeps the steps at Werner's Grocery on Oshkosh Avenue
Photo Credit: Dan Radig, FB

GROCERY STORES

The neighborhood grocer was the "unsung hero" of those times since it was they who looked after their neighbors, especially during World War II and The Great Depression. These merchants provided much needed food to families even when at times they didn't have the means to pay. Many debts were "forgiven" back then. That's just the way it was. People looked after one another.

The 1950's saw a change in the grocery business with the onset of the supermarket. As a child I have early memories of the Krambo store on Jackson, Food Queen and National on Main and Oregon Streets, Red Owl on Murdock, Piggly Wiggly on Ohio and Murdock Streets and Stangel's Super Valu on Sawyer Street. Bucky Walters operated what was then known as "The Largest Supermarket on New York Avenue"...Bucky's Food Town. Copps on Hwy 41, just south of Ninth Avenue was the first store of its kind that offered both hard goods and groceries; a prelude to today's WalMart concept. Half the store was dedicated to a "department store" concept while the other half a fully stocked supermarket. In the mid 60's, Kmart on Koeller Ave remodeled and added a Red Owl grocery store into their business.

As these big stores started to emerge, slowly, the Mom and Pop stores started to disappear. These new stores were large and modern, offering the convenience of a large variety of dry goods, fresh meats and produce, bakery, dairy and frozen foods. It was here, and then, that I started my career in the grocery business.

Above: Food Queen; Right: Nielsen's; both on Main St.
Photo Credits: Dan Radig

Stangel's Super Valu

It was 1965. I was 14 years old and like many boys my age, looking for a way to earn some money. Cutting lawns in the summer and shoveling snow (yes shoveling, no snow blower then) in winter were a couple of ways to earn some spending money, but not much. I was collecting baseball cards in the early 1960's and would buy a pack of 5 cards for a nickel...relying on the occasional handout from my Mom. The stale piece of gum was good for only a few minutes, then quickly dispatched as I rifled through my pack of childhood heroes with great anticipation looking for those coveted Milwaukee Braves cards. Aaron, Mathews, Spahn and Burdette...they were my boyhood heroes of summer.

The Stangel Family opened a Super Valu store on Sawyer Street and Southland Avenue, two blocks east of my house on Lark St. Danny Stangel was one of the Stangel brothers who managed the store. Danny took customer service to a new high. He would greet customers as he made his way around the store. "Hi there...hello...how ya doin? He'd say, sometimes from half an aisle away; never pausing to hear or expect a response.

In the mid 60's, the Stangel family sold the store to Ed Prescott. Ed, his wife Ruth and their eight children had just moved to Oshkosh from Iowa and were looking to make a start with a business of their own.

Ed and his trademark suspenders worked to become the busiest supermarket in town. Ed was a working owner. By that, I mean he did everything; stocked shelves, unloaded trucks, opened a checkout when it got busy, carried customers groceries out to the car, ran to bank, did the bookkeeping...he did it all! One day Ed noticed a woman with a couple of bags of groceries asking for someone to call her a taxi. Ed pulled his white station wagon up to the front door, loaded her grocery bags into the back seat, and gave her a ride home. His wife Ruth was right there with him managing office functions, manning the customer service desk, bookkeeping, banking, checkouts, etc. They were a team.

So, where was I? Oh yes...the year is 1965 and I'm 14 years old...

I would ride my bike down to the store almost every day, since I lived only two blocks away. I would walk through the double set of glass doors that opened automatically when you stepped on the "magic mat", and proceeded to the "courtesy counter" where Ed and Ruth were perched and ran the store's business operations. The counter was near the front door and allowed them to watch over the check stands. As soon as there were more than a few people in line, Ed or Ruth would hustle over, open another register, and get customers quickly on their way.

As I walked up to the counter, Ed always greeted me with a little smile and said "Helloooooo Randy...how ya doin today?" I flashed back with a smile and asked if he had any openings for me. "How old are you?" he would ask. "Fourteen", I answered back. "Well, when you turn fifteen, you come back and see me", he said, and then turned back to his work.

Not to be deterred, I would walk through the store until I found Jack Beck. Jack was a full time stocker and assistant manager, and would one day become a store manager for Ed. I would find Jack stocking shelves or filling the frozen food cases. After emptying each case, he would rip the cardboard carton down each corner, flatten the box and put it in an empty grocery basket. On occasion, he would let me rip boxes for him and then… my favorite part…take the cardboard to the backroom, put it in the incinerator and burn it. (This was before recycling was a big deal).

This scenario went on for some time. I never got paid for any of my efforts but I didn't care. Once in awhile, Jack would buy me a soda or give me a doughnut from the bakery. Good enough!

On July 29, 1966 I turned fifteen years old.

That day I rode my bike to the store, as usual, strolled up to the courtesy counter and said "Ed…it's my birthday today! I'm fifteen!" Ed looked at me over his glasses and said "Is that so? Well, you know if you want to work at fifteen, you're going to need to get a work permit". Another delay tactic I presumed. Then Ed explained it was law, and I needed to go down to the courthouse and apply for a work permit. I went back home and told my Mom. She agreed to take me there that afternoon.

The next day I walked into the store and presented my permit proudly to Ed. He looked at it and said "OK…follow me". He led me to the back room, handed me a bucket, a squeegee and a rag. We walked outside to the end of the long glass pane windows that framed the storefront. He showed me the proper technique on window washing and how not to leave streaks. I caught on rather quickly.

It was only a short time later that I knew I had a really cool job. Shirley Cushman was the head checker. It was getting busy when Shirley grabbed the PA attached to her check stand and announced to the world…"RANDY CARRYOUT PLEASE". I was famous! I hustled up front and started to bag a customers groceries. When the order was completely bagged, I grabbed my cart, loaded it with the bags full of groceries I had just neatly packed and proudly followed the customer to her car! That was a great day!!!

I spent the next few years fine tuning my skills as a "bagboy". I quickly learned that bakery goes on top, frozen foods got double bagged and "…not to pack the bags too heavy, young man, unless you're going to come home and carry them in the house for me".

From bagger I learned to work other jobs in the store. As a stock boy, we had to learn how to unload the truck, properly cut the cases with a box cutter without cutting into the product inside, price mark and organize the cases in preparation for stocking the shelves. As a vacation fill-in, I worked in the Produce department, trimming and wrapping lettuce, packaging apples and oranges and the sort. My favorite time working produce came in the summer months when the watermelon trucks would arrive from Texas. We set up an assembly line of sorts and one-by-one tossed melons from the hay-lined bed in the back of the open backed semi trailer. Usually the salty old driver would climb into the cab and sleep while we unloaded the truck. "Wake me up when you're finished" he would say with that drawn out Texas drawl and then disappear into the cab, not to be seen for a couple hours.

In 1970, Karen and I were married and we started our family. The salary for a stock boy in a grocery store was not enough to support a young family. One day, Ed approached me and said he had a position open in the meat department. I would need to complete an apprenticeship on meat cutting over the next 30 months. The meat jobs were the only union jobs in the store and the pay was much better than I was making as it was skilled labor, a real trade, so I agreed to it.

Grocery Stores

I learned to cut meat from the team of experienced butchers that worked in the store. Milton "Shorty" Thiele was the meat manager while Jack Baldridge and Herb Brunover were the two seasoned cutters who taught me the trade. I completed my 30 month apprenticeship in 1973 and earned the trade title "Journeyman Meat Cutter".

Ed Prescott, owner of Sawyer Street Super Valu bags up an order while checker Shirley Cushman looks on

Baldridge became the meat manager when Shorty retired and ran the department until the store was sold in 1981. Jack was originally from Texas and liked to tell tales of his youth as a Texan. Herbie had a keen sense of humor and always had a joke or humorous remark ready at a moment's notice. Our meat wrappers were Patricia Youngwirth (Shorty's daughter), Loretta Perry and Judy Stertz. The names and faces changed over the years, but this was "the crew" in my early years working at the store. Ticker Reichenberger also worked with us for a few years after the Reichenberger family closed their own store on 6th and Knapp Street.

YESTERDAY IN OSHKOSH...MY HOMETOWN

Ed takes a minute to check with a couple of "future customers" to ensure they are having a good shopping experience

Photo Credits: Dan Radig, Ed and August Tiedje

Owner Ed Prescott looks on as the author Randy Domer demonstrates expert meat cutting skills ...Meat Manager Milton "Shorty" Thiele supervises. Circa 1971

Those were wonderful times. The people at Sawyer Street Supervalu were like family. I worked in that store, for the Prescott family, until December, 1985.

Sawyer Street Super Valu was a family owned and operated business. (Left Photo) Owner Ed Prescott discusses business with son George (left) and son-in-law Howard Locke (center). (Right Photo) Ed chats with one the regular customers while Ken Grenz bags up the order

Photo Credits: Ed and August Tiedje, Dan Radig

Oshkosh's Very Own...

MARK GRUENWALD

"LOOK! Up in the sky! Is it a bird?...Is it a plane?...NO! It's Superman!"

"Faster than a speeding bullet...more powerful than a locomotive..."

It was all about comic books.

That's how I became friends with Mark Gruenwald. Mark lived on Sawyer Street, across the street from Mars drive in. Mark was two years younger than me, but we both shared an interest in one thing...The Justice League of America (JLA).

I was twelve years old at the time when Mark came up with this great idea. "Let's form our own club of The JLA!" If you're not familiar with the Justice League, it was created by DC comics and was a consortium of "Super Heroes" banding together, dedicated to fight evil. Superman, Batman, Green Lantern, Flash, Wonder Woman, J'onn J'onzz, Aquaman, and Green Arrow made up most of the original team. Mark had a terrific comic book collection as did I. At the time, I worked hard to scrape up some money every week or two to buy a couple comics at the Mueller Potter drugstore on Oshkosh Ave. When I first started buying comics, they were 10 cents each. Then in time the price rose to 12 cents and then 15 cents.

We would ride our bikes to Mueller Potter and stand at the magazine rack located in the front window and in the southwest corner of the store. We spent what seemed like hours paging through comics; so many choices as each super hero also had their own comic as well. Eventually, I would decide on which one or two I wanted, then made my way to the back of store where my friend's mother waited to check us out. Mike Lichtenwald's mom, Jeanette, worked at Mueller Potter for many years. Mrs. Lichtenwald would ring us up and off we would go, heading home to read the latest adventure. (Regretfully, Mrs. Jeanette Lichtenwald passed away during the writing of this book)

So, Mark started the club and offered the use of his garage attic as the clubhouse. Since it was his idea and he was providing the clubhouse, Mark got to be Superman. Neighbor Keith Boushele was Batman, my cousin Lee Ziebell was Aquaman, Mark's younger sister Gail became Wonder Woman, and his neighbor Jeff Paffenroth was The Flash. Me? *I was the Green Lantern*! Costumes were made as we played out our character roles.

The author as The Green Lantern; circa 1963
Photo Credit: Randy Domer

As we grew up, our interests changed and the JLA slowly gave way to other childhood interests. That is, for most of us.

Mark's passion for super heroes and adventure never waned. In the 1970's Mark wrote text articles for DC Comics and in 1978 at age 25, Mark became an assistant editor with Marvel Comics.

Mark continued to advance his career with Marvel and was promoted to Executive Editor by the late 1980's. An interesting note: Mark was renowned for his memory of details. In fact, Marvel created a contest where fans would write in and try to stump Mark on obscure details from past issues and character backgrounds. After some time, they decided to end the contest as Mark would never lose.

Mark held various titles working at Marvel over the years: a writer, assistant editor, editor, editor-in-chief, executive editor, and colorist. His work covered many of the popular super heroes including Captain America, Thor, Spiderman, The Avengers, The Fantastic Four, The Hulk and countless others.

Mark quickly earned the reputation as the "self appointed morale ambassador" at Marvel Comics. He was a practical joker and always capable of the unexpected. His endless supply of optimism and enthusiasm for comics was evidenced by his involvement with organizing company picnics; Halloween parties and gets credit for creating the Marvel Olympics featured at comic conventions across the country.

Sadly, Mark succumbed to an untimely death, suffering a heart attack in 1996 at the age of 43. It was reported that just days prior to his death, Mark was doing one of his trademark cartwheels down the hall at work, much to the delight of his coworkers. Because of his reputation as a practical joker, it's been said that his co-workers, upon hearing the news, believed this was just another of Mark's pranks.

It is here, though, that this story takes a strange twist.

In the writing of his last will and testament, Mark had made a special request. His desire, after his death, was to be cremated and have his ashes mixed with printing ink, and used to publish a comic compilation of his work.

His request was honored by his family and with the blessing and assistance of Marvel Comics, Marks ashes were used in the publication of a paperback edition of *Squadron Supreme*. The edition contained a statement regarding Marks "direct involvement" and the first printing

Mark Gruenwald with his hero..Captain America
Photo Credit: Marvel Comics

sold out very quickly. Subsequent issues where then printed, but with the disclaimer "without ashes".

Marks story was recently featured on the Discovery Channel on a program called "Strange Last Requests." Mark's wife Catherine joined the taping and recounted the story in her own words. Mark has gone on to be memorialized in later editions of Marvel comics. One issue refers to a building in Gotham City as the "Von Gruenwald Tower", while another features a character, a lawyer named Mark Gruenwald, who has similar physical characteristics of Mark and plays a heroic role throughout the story.

In the end, Mark truly fulfilled his lifelong dream…to literally **be** in the comics he loved so dearly.

Home Delivery - 1950's Style

Today, we can use the convenience of the internet to order everything from groceries to furniture and it will be delivered right to our door. But home delivery is not something new. In the mid 1950's, pickup trucks full of produce would cruise the neighborhoods, offering fresh home grown sweet corn, strawberries and various other garden fresh vegetables that were in season. In fall, the trucks would be loaded with different varieties of fresh picked apples by the bag or by the bushel. Squash and pumpkins would be piled high on the bed of these old beat up pickups. It was the farmers' means of transportation and distribution all in one. And the best part...no middle man.

One of my favorite memories growing up was that of our milkman. In the 1950's, most people had one of the local dairies deliver fresh milk and assorted dairy products right to their door. Some of the local dairies included Cowan's, Fahrnwald Farms, Carver's and GDC... just to name a few.

The Guernsey Dairy Company, or GDC as we all knew it, was the largest dairy in town and the bottling plant was located at State and Otter Streets , just one block east of downtown Main Street.

I remember my favorites: Chocolate milk, Orange Drink, Half and Half, Cottage Cheese with Chives and Creamy Top Milk. The Creamy Top Milk came in a special bottle. It was somewhat square shaped from the bottom up; with a neck that separated the bottom part from a bulbous shaped top. The bottle was sealed with a cardboard stopper and a green colored cellophane wrapper. What made this product unique was the shape of the bottle. It allowed the cream in the high fat milk to rise to the top and separate from the rest of the milk. You could insert a little stopper that closed off the neck, and pour just the

Home Delivery - 1950's Style

DEPENDABLE FRESHNESS EVERY TIME

IT WHIPS

GDC

Never In Doubt!

Whether At Your Store or Your Door

It pays to trade with folks you know

cream off, if you wish. Or, if you choose, you could just shake the bottle up before opening and mix the cream back into the milk.

In school, we paid ten cents a week to get our milk each day. If you forgot to bring your "*milk money*" to school, you went without. The milk was served in half pint size glass bottles with the GDC logo printed on the side.

The delivery route for GDC along Lark Street belonged to Orv Baier. Orv was our milkman for many years. On delivery day, Orv would pull his orange and white GDC refrigerated delivery van in front of our house. Dressed in the typical milkman attire of the trademark Oshkosh B'Gosh pinstriped bib overalls and matching cap, Orv went about his rounds.

At our back door sat the silver metal milk box with the reddish orange GDC logo emblazoned on the front. It was insulated (somewhat) to keep your milk cold until you could fetch it and put it in your refrigerator. Orv would pull up in his truck, which, by the way, he drove standing up. The door, if there was one, was always open, which allowed him to quickly jump in and out as he made his rounds. He carried a wire basket that held approximately six containers of milk. That way, he could deliver to two or more houses before returning to his truck to reload.

I'm sure it was against the rules, but on occasion, Orv would let us hop in the truck and ride part way down the street with him. That was serious fun when I was seven years old!

A GDC Milkman making his morning delivery
Photo Credit: Ed and August Tiedje

By the mid to late 1960's, as supermarkets started popping up across town, home milk delivery started to fade away. Orv's duties now included delivering milk and dairy products to the Sawyer Street Super Valu that I worked in. I was married now and a number of years had passed, but Orv still remembered me. I was cutting meat and once in awhile he would poke his head into the meat cooler and say "Hey Randy...want a quart of Chocolate Milk?" One particular year, it was mid-afternoon on Christmas Eve. Orv had made his final delivery to the store and was done for the day, and ready to go home and enjoy the holiday with his family. My co-workers and I were cleaning up and ready to punch out and go home ourselves, when Orv walked behind the meat case and into the cutting room. In his hand was a pint of Aristocrat Brandy. You see, people took care of the milkman, the postman, etc. during the holidays with a little token of appreciation of a job well done throughout the year. In his other hand was a quart of GDC's finest eggnog. He poured some of the brandy into the cardboard carton, gave it a good shake, and then poured us each a little glass. He raised his cup and toasted us one and all, "Merry Christmas fellas." Down the hatch, a few handshakes and pats on the back and we all went our own ways.

Orv Baier passed away on June 15, 2006. He was 89 years old. He is gone now, but surely not forgotten.

THE ATHEARN

As I was considering the numerous topics to cover in this book, I decided it needed to include the historic Athearn Hotel. Each time we went to the Grand Theater, the Athearn was the first thing we saw as we exited the theater. Although I was pretty young at the time, I clearly remember that stately hotel that stood so proudly in Monument Square. I was visiting the Grand recently, and as I walked out of the opera house onto Algoma and look toward Monument Square, a part of me still expects to see it there today. But, to my dismay, I only see an Auto Bank and parking lot where the majestic old hotel once stood.

Because of my age, I didn't feel I had enough background on the Athearn to do this chapter justice, so I turned to my friend, Jim Senderhauf for assistance. Jim is eight years my senior and often talked about the days he spent inside the Athearn. His memories were clear and vivid about the people who worked there, the clientele and the interior layout.

I decided Jim was better suited to write this chapter, and when I approached him with the idea, he quickly agreed.

Here is Jim's story…

The Athearn
By James Senderhauf

The Athearn was built in 1891 by a visionary by the name of George Athearn. Some say it surpassed any of the turn of the century hotels in Milwaukee which probably was debatable back then but it certainly was the most elegant of hotels north of Milwaukee and the crown jewel of Oshkosh, Wisconsin. It was a great addition to the city and complemented the Grand Opera House offering superb lodging to famous people performing at the

Opera House and many dignitaries and travelers visiting an early Oshkosh.

My recollections of the Athearn are from the 1950's. In 1952 the hotel was purchased by 3 sisters, Margaret and Ann McCaffery and Jeanne McCaffery Hall from Wabasha, Minnesota. This triage of hotel expertise was raised in the hotel industry where their Grandma Belle Anderson along with their mother ran a well-known Minnesota hotel called the Anderson House. The Anderson House was known in Minnesota for its feats of culinary excellence served in the Anderson House dining room. The 3 sisters wasted no time in bringing this type of atmosphere to the Athearn.

James Senderhauf

After my mother passed away my dad met Jeanne Hall and in 1956 they were married. What a change in the life of a 13 year old Oshkosh native. During that era, it was unusual to have women running a business let alone be the proprietors of an Oshkosh icon. Growing up I remember seeing the Athearn, but don't remember ever having been inside. I remember the day my Dad took my brother and me to the Athearn to meet Jeanne for the first time. I had never given any thought to what the inside of the Athearn might look like and was never exposed to any place elegant enough to impress me. Previous to this day, I had never been in a hotel in my life.

I still remember the awesome feeling that came over me when we stepped foot in the lobby. The polished carved woodwork and leather furniture along with the guests of the hotel sitting and talking or standing at the front desk being checked in is an image in a 13 year old brain that still has a place in my mind 56 years later. After the lobby the next adventure was the elevator. The elevator operator greeted my dad by name, and then dad introduced us to him. I don't remember his name but I remember what he said. "Hello boys, I hear we will be seeing more of you two here soon". It was then the significance of this meeting started to sink in. Jeanne had a suite in the hotel and the take away memory I have was the wall to wall book shelves, completely filled. She was a voracious reader and an elegant host to her soon to be new family.

That evening, we had dinner in the English Room. To me this was like eating in a castle and a far cry from the Friday night fish fries in neighborhood taverns that had been my previous dining experience. We spent many more nights eating in the English Room and its elegance never ceased to amaze me. The floors were marble and decorative. The ceilings beamed with polished wood, tables adorned with fine, white linen tablecloths and napkins, gleaming heavy silverware placed perfectly at each table setting. At one end of the room, a huge, ornate fireplace added to the ambiance. The entire room was lit by beautiful crystal chandeliers. It was an impressive and well remembered first day.

My Dad and Jeanne were married for 7 years before divorcing and those 7 years and my recollection of the Athearn is what this chapter is about.

To know the Athearn during this time it is important the expertise

The Athearn Hotel 1964
Photo Credit: Dan Radig, Ed Tiedje

and talents of the three sisters be understood and documented. They were smart, personable, and very capable of running a hotel. Each of them were college educated and had grown up studied and trained in the hotel business. Jeanne and Ann were experts in the culinary field and Margaret was the authority in the hotel operations and housekeeping part of the business. After the Athearn closed Jeanne and Margaret had successful careers. Margaret became Margaret Kappa when she married Nick Kappa while living in Oshkosh. She wrote several books on Hotel Housekeeping that are still available today. She became the Executive Housekeeper for the prestigious Greenbrier Resort in West Virginia and then served as a consultant for the Grand Hotel on Mackinac Island for 20 years, where she had a home. All 3 of the sisters are now passed away.

After Jeanne and my dad were married, I learned how really talented Jeanne was. I observed her at the Athearn and also in the house we had moved in to. She put in long hours, leaving the house mid morning and sometimes not returning home until later at night. At the hotel she was a dynamo and, from what I could tell, people working there respected and liked her. She was demanding but fair. All three of the sisters commanded perfection. I also learned that her hobby was writing and she was very successful at entering contests writing about food and winning great prizes. She won 2 cars which she sold, a diamond studded men's watch and gift certificates from Nieman Marcus to name a few. After the Athearn, she managed the Town Grill in Oshkosh and changed the name to the Town House. She then went on to manage a chain of hotels and we visited some of these in Venice, Florida; Biloxi, Mississippi; and Duluth, Minnesota. After this, she worked for the Green Bay Packer organization, where my brother and dad dined with the Packer team of the Bart Starr/Vince Lombardi era at their training camp at Saint Norbert College in DePere, Wisconsin. She was then employed by the Playboy organization and was in charge of planning many events at the Playboy mansion in Chicago. Eventually, she went back to her roots and took over ownership of the Anderson Hotel in Wabasha, Minnesota.

My best recollection of the daily activities of the Athearn is for a period of time in 1959 when I worked as a part time elevator operator. The Athearn, during this period, was a bustling and lively place. There always seemed to be something going on. The mornings were busy with some guests checking out while other guests enjoyed a quiet breakfast. The meeting rooms hosted some of the breakfasts and activities for the morning businesses and organizations that met at that time. During the lull in the morning between the breakfast and lunch period, the hotel employees were still busy. The maids at the hotel scurried to make up rooms to prepare for returning guests and new ones checking in. Margaret was a professional and everything had to be perfect. I can remember her inspecting the rooms and hallways of the floors to make sure everything was ready. The dining rooms were transformed and made ready for noon meetings and lunch. The waitresses and bus boys were busy and Jeanne's watchful eye was ever present to make sure place settings were perfectly placed and napkins folded correctly. After every room was ready she would stand back and look over the room, making any final adjustments to ensure guests entering a room to dine did not see anything out of place or anything else that would suggest that their meal would be less than perfect.

The English Room was the focal point for the evening meal. The menu was unlike any in Oshkosh. There was the traditional steaks and seafood along with special dishes. The special dishes were sometimes given names preceded by family member names like "Aunt Belle" and "Grandma Anderson", letting the customers know that these were special family recipes that were created just for them. I remember the best steaks were more expensive than the lobster. The expensive cuts of steak were over $4.00 for a meal and the one pound African Lobster with drawn butter was $3.95. This included dessert. Best remembered are the homemade pecan and fudge pies. I was allowed to bring a friend to the Athearn a few times to share a meal. I remember signing the bill and adding a10% tip. The soups were also special kitchen creations. The waitresses were always dressed to perfection. The employee's attire and uniforms was constantly monitored and employees knew that if they were not perfectly dressed and coifed their appearance would be addressed.

On Saturday nights the English Room was transformed into some theme to make a night out an event to remember. The Saturday Night "Chuck Wagon Buffet" and "Plantation Nights" were the favorites. Buffets were not common back then so these were popular and well attended. For any theme night the staff was dressed in the style of the theme. For the Chuck Wagon Buffet they were dressed in western garb and the scrumptious buffet table ended with a "cowboy" carving a huge prime rib roast and adding it to a customer's already full plate. On Plantation Night they switched to a southern atmosphere and the employees were dressed as help from a Southern Plantation. The food was always the drawing card at any meal in the English Room. Everything had to be perfect. I heard Jeanne tell her sister once that the food is only as good as the appearance of the dining room and those who serve it. The steak knives always had to be sharp as Jeanne often would say "The best cut of meat could be judged as tough because of a dull knife".

The kitchen, before meal preparation began, was spotless from the efforts of those who helped close down the night before. Once the preparation of meals started it became a place to "stay out of the way". Evening meals were the most exciting to observe, especially when there were special events. Everyone had a job and to observe the scurrying around made it difficult to see how anyone got served their meal.

The Athearn in Monument Square
Photo Credit: Ed and August Tiedje

Before the dining room opened, there was a crew that prepared for the meals. There were salad girls cleaning and cutting the vegetables for the salads, potatoes were being peeled, and cooks were preparing food that could be made ahead of time under the watchful eye of head chef Al "Shorty" Piotter. Jeanne held him in high regard and gave him much of the credit for the tasty dishes the Athearn was known for. She hired Piotter because of his wonderful reputation for years working at The Peacock Restaurant. He was always a busy person in the kitchen and totally in charge.

It impressed me to see all of the unused greens from the vegetables put into a huge pot on the stove filled with hot water. After this concoction had been simmered long enough two of the cooks would grab this huge pot and 2 others would unfold a large piece of cheese cloth over another pot. The contents of the greens would then be strained out of the liquid and that would become stock for some of the great soups the Athearn were known for. Once the orders for the meals started coming in it fascinated me that what appeared to me to be mass confusion was actually very well organized and as always the food went out on time and was always perfect.

The social area of the Athearn was the Gay Nineties Bar. I never was allowed to spend a lot of time in there but I remember it well. It seemed constantly busy at night and was a great place for people to come and have a drink and socialize with friends. Occasionally they had lounge entertainers that would be brought in for listening enjoyment. There was a customer favorite, a couple named "Bob and Marie" and when they came to Oshkosh they always drew a crowd. Marie was not only beautiful but had a powerful voice that could be heard throughout the building when she sang. I remember her closing song was "Until There Was You". She would hit every note perfectly and would bring a standing ovation and an encore. They asked me to join them for lunch one time and told me about their travels to different cities. I learned what an agent was and that they had one. They told me they had visited almost every state. I was mesmerized by their life style. They remained popular and were featured at the Athearn quite often.

Another well traveled place was the barbershop. It was located down a set of stairs in the lobby and leased to Bud BonEsse. There were many barbershops located around Main Street in Oshkosh, but judging by the men who patronized the Athearn barbershop, his was one of the most popular. He catered to the businessmen and I would wait my turn, which sometimes was taken by one of the adults who came in after me. Bud, like all good barbers back then, kept the conversation going and seemed to be in the know on many of the things happening in the city. The men were always dressed in suits and a tie and always looked important. I don't recall what the cost of a haircut was back then, but I was given a dollar by my dad and instructed to tell him to keep the change. There was also a beauty parlor in the Athearn, and a laundry and dry cleaning service available for guests if they needed it.

The Athearn had a number of suites that housed several permanent residents. There were two brothers who each had their own connecting suites and were well known in Oshkosh. They owned Kline's Department Store on Main Street. I remember the Kline brothers as being quiet and friendly. The other resident I remembered was Dolly Athearn. She was a daughter-in-law to George Athearn. She was a very sophisticated looking lady always very well dressed. She spent a lot of time in the lobby and I wish now I had taken the time to get to know her better. She was friendly and I always felt she was a lonesome lady. She would sit by a window and seemed to be content in her thoughts and memories of having lived there for over fifty years. Both Dolly and the Kline brothers were able to park their cars in the Athearn garage which was located at the back of the hotel. Space was limited and it was used by the three sisters, Dolly, and the Kline brothers. I parked there many times and the garage had a door leading to the basement. This was a fascinating place because of the furniture and other treasures from years gone by stored there. It had huge wooden beams for rafters and to leave the basement you had to weave your way underneath the entire building until you came to a door across from the barber shop and from there up the stairs to the lobby. It was like leaving a haunted house and finding civilization.

There was an unfinished part of the Athearn called the Annex. It was built with the idea it could be finished as expanded business would create a need for more rooms. It was heated, and the community bathrooms that were shared by guests were operable. Enrollment was expanding at the university in Oshkosh and for a few years, the Annex became the home for attending college students. It was a novel place and those that lived there could write their own stories on what went on there. Back then, the girls' dorms had curfew hours and the boys' dorms didn't. The theory was that if the girls had to go home, the boys would too. But if the walls to the annex could talk, it would attest that this theory didn't always work and hours were not always followed.

The demise of the Athearn started a few years before it was actually torn down. In conversations I remember hearing, revenue and cash flow were becoming a problem. The rooms of the Athearn were traditional hotel rooms with few having private baths. They needed to be renovated, but even if that money was spent, the patterns of where travelers ended up for the night were changing. More people were traveling by car and going to the center of town for lodging was falling out of vogue. Motels were springing up along the US 41 corridor on the west edge of town. In these new motels, every room had a private bath and shower. You could drive and park right in front of your room. Some were even putting in swimming pools and many had television sets in the room and air conditioning. I remember rates at the Athearn being around $5/day. A motel room could be rented out for about the same price. The University was also building large new dorms and the need to rent the annex would go away. On top of that, I remember my Dad telling me that an even bigger problem was that it was going to cost too much money to get the Athearn to comply with structural problems that were surfacing. Plumbing, electrical and heating all needed to be replaced. There were even more demands to be up to code. The wood in the flooring had to be replaced with steel.

In 1962 Jeanne and her sisters left the Athearn and the writing was on the wall signaling the end was not only near, but inevitable.

Should the Athearn have been saved? If it had been left standing would the elegant lady have transformed into what the Grand Opera House was back then… left to run down and disgrace its history? Back then the city was into modernization not preservation. As it was, the Athearn stood majestically and with honor, looking toward Main Street for all to see her as an elegant lady, preserving her dignity, right up to the end.

Authors Notes:

The Athearn was designed by renowned architect William Waters and constructed by C.R. Meyer and Sons (a three year old company at the time). The Athearn was built at the estimated cost of $100,000 to

$125,000 and intended to give Oshkosh, the second largest city in the state, a hostelry suited for a city of this size.

The Athearn "attracted many famous people in its 73 year history." In 1912, "Former President Teddy Roosevelt spoke in Oshkosh and had dinner that evening at the Athearn. The game laws were suspended for the evening and the feature of the meal was roast mallard duck". (Source: Prairie, Pines and People, pg 381, Oshkosh Daily Northwestern, James Metz)

William Howard Taft, Clarence Darrow, William Jennings Bryan and Maude Adams all visited and also dined there. Duke Ellington's band visited the Gay Nineties bar one evening and gave a standing ovation to the local entertainers". (Source: Oshkosh Northwestern, December 16, 1984)

George Athearn and his wife Eliza ran the hotel until 1944 then sold it to Mr. and Mrs. Thomas Kewley. In 1952, the Kewleys offered the hotel for long-term lease with option to buy and the McCaffrey sisters took over.

A 1893 publication titled "Pen and Sunlight Sketches of the Principle Cities in Wisconsin", published by Phoenix Publishing Company, Chicago, IL (Source: Oshkosh Public Library) reported the following:

THE ATHEARN HOTEL

The most popular hotel in this part of the State of Wisconsin is the Athearn Hotel at Oshkosh. It is at the corner of High and Market streets, and was opened in May, 1891. It was built and is owned by the Oshkosh Hotel Company, the building costing $125,000, and was planned by one of the best architects of the state, Mr. William Waters. It is built of pressed brick with white sandstone trimmings, and consists of four stories and a large, commodious basement. The cost for furnishing this palatial establishment was $40,000, which was borne by Mr. Athearn, its present proprietor. It has 180 feet frontage on Market Street, and extends back for 120 feet, and has two elevators. It is heated by steam, lighted by electricity, has electric bells and all modern conveniences The flooring is of mosaic tiles, while all the rooms throughout are finished in antique oak. Two dining rooms are included, an ordinary dining room, and one arranged for the private use of the regular boarders. These dining halls will seat comfortably one hundred *and fifty persons and are both located upon the ground floor. A bar, stocked with the choicest liquors, wines and drinks of all sorts is one of the prominent features, while a billiard room, reading room and writing room supply all the possible needs of the guests. A telegraph station is also within its domains, while lady stenographers, the most expert of hotel clerks and bookkeepers are in the employ of this great establishment. The Athearn Hotel is run upon the American plan, the rates being from $2 to $4.50 per day. Seventy-five guest chambers are handsomely furnished and equipped. Mr. G. W. Athearn, Sr., was born in Maine and is a middle aged gentleman. He has lived in Oshkosh for twenty-five years, and was formerly the proprietor of the Revere House of this city, while previous to that Mr. Athearn had charge of and owned the Palmer House of Fond du Lac.*

An article in The Daily Northwestern dated October 7, 1930 states… *"With its 160 rooms, all modern, it is the mecca for the tourists, the resting place for tired travelers who are seeking the ultimate in accommodations. Sixty rooms with baths, large sized sample rooms, and an unusual cuisine serve as an advertisement for Oshkosh that is known throughout the breadth of the land.*

So, since it was built in 1891, by 1930 The Athearn expanded its room capacity from 75 to 160 rooms

When C.R. Meyer built the Athearn in 1891, Oshkosh was a major lumber center. The hotel's frame was therefore made of wood, an abundant and cheap commodity, with brick overlay. This, in addition to the oak beamed ceilings and oak floors, made the hotel a "firetrap" 73 years after it was built. To meet building codes in the 1960's, the wood structure would have to be replaced with steel. (Source: Oshkosh Northwestern, December16, 1984)

On December 29, 1964, the Oshkosh Daily Northwestern reported construction crews had moved in to begin the demolition process. The caption beneath what was to be one of the last photographs of the Athearn read, *"Athearn Stands Through Last Holiday Season"*. The sub caption then went on almost like an obituary, stating *"Its awning still hospitably extended the 75-year-old Athearn Hotel waits this holiday season for a wrecking crew. Once the scene of the city's gayest gatherings, the Athearn echoed only to the sounds of workmen during its last holiday season. Berg & Henn crews rigged a giant crane Monday on Commerce Street, just off High Avenue, ready to begin demolition this week. The site will be cleared for a New American Bank, a major step in revitalizing the city's downtown center."*

The wrecking ball then did its work to bring another historic landmark down. The rubble and remnants from The Athearn were used as landfill on Ki-Ni Island to build the Pioneer Inn, which too has since met its demise.

Today, the Athearn lives on in the memories of Jim Senderhauf and others like him who were touched by her beauty and elegance.

The Legion on the Lake

Located at the end of Washington Avenue, "The Legion" as it was commonly referred to by the locals, hosted everything from wedding receptions to high school dances and everything else in between. This Oshkosh landmark has been the site of many important events for over a century.

Occupied off and on through the decades by both The American Legion and the Oshkosh Yacht Club, I knew there was much more to the story than my research was uncovering. I decided to contact Bill Wyman who with his wife Beth purchased the historic mansion in 2007. Bill quickly accepted my offer to meet and talk about the storied legacy of this estate.

It was a bright beautiful morning, gentle waves from Lake Winnebago lapping the shores as I drove into the parking lot and pulled up nearest to the building. I noted the lot was empty except for a few cars of staff members and a number of seagulls competing for a discarded item I couldn't identify. I climbed out of my car and started heading for the door when a voice called to me. I turned to see it was owner Bill Wyman, busily working to untangle some garden hoses near the maintenance building located on the south end of the property. As Bill walked toward me, I was greeted by his two Bearded Collies, Harry and Genevieve.

Bill greeted me with a firm handshake and commented on how many little things there always seem to be when you have a property of this size to look after. As he wiped his hands, he invited me to follow him as he walked toward the side entrance of the mansion. The morning sun lit up the stately white building and I was struck by its beauty as I started to understand why it's preservation was so important. He stuck the key in the lock and opened the door, calling for Harry and Genevieve to follow us inside.

Our path took us through the kitchen area and into the bar area where we chose a table for our meeting. The porch area where we sat is lined with large windows, affording a lovely view of Lake Winnebago. The sun's rays were bright and filled the east facing room with both light and warmth. After some initial introductions we quickly got down to business.

Bill's expression lit up as started to tell me about the early history of the estate. He explained that in the early 1900's, the vacant property here was owned by local architect William Waters.

"*The Richard Harney residence stood at the foot of Washington Boulevard, on the shore of Lake Winnebago. He had purchased his home from Mr. and Mrs. Peter McCourt, who had been presented with it by their daughter, Mrs. Horace Austin Warner Tabor* (better known today as Oshkosh's born and raised Baby Doe Tabor) *of Leadville and Denver, Colorado. Baby Doe Tabor's bonanza king husband had struck it rich in Colorado silver and she shared her good fortune with her parents back east.*"

"*Thereafter, in the flow of events, a prominent Oshkosh Architect, William Waters (the designer of the Grand Opera House) acquired the property for the Yacht Club at a cost of $9,000, $3,000 of which was to be paid immediately and the rest by terms of a promissory note for six years at 5% interest per annum. Payments were made twice a year: $500 on January 1 and July 1.*"

Source: 1869-1969, a century of sail on Winnebago; The Centennial Yearbook of the Oshkosh Yacht Club, James A. Young, Editor

On April 23, 1903, William Waters being an avid sportsman donated the property to the Oshkosh Yacht Club. The OYC, established in 1869, did not have a property of their own and was renting space at the foot of Bay Street, next to the Northwestern Railroad Bridge where the club built only a harbor and wharf. The OYC used Dickensen's Boathouse as their headquarters until about 1886, then for the next 11 years the club meetings were held at the Athearn Hotel. The OYC wanted to build a new clubhouse and agreed to the stipulation from Mr. Waters and his generous donation that he would design it.

William Waters is renowned for some of Oshkosh's most magnificent and storied landmarks. His talent for architecture is evident in such places as the Grand Opera House, the Public Library, the Oshkosh

Public Museum (formerly the Sawyer Mansion), the Athearn Hotel and Brooklyn Firehouse, are just a few among many.

The stately mansion was built in only three months time for the Oshkosh Yacht Club, which hosted annual regattas that drew people from all over the country. Steamships and excursion boats would anchor in front of the "Legion", while the balconies and lawn were filled with observers watching the races on the beautiful waters of Lake Winnebago.

The new OYC clubhouse, originally built as a summer building with no heat, was an exciting and significant event for the city back then.

Building costs, financed largely by donations from 600 Yacht Club members, were estimated to be $10,000, but by the time the project was complete, overruns raised the final cost to $12,000 not including furnishings or fixtures.

In 1903 the city buzzed with excitement about the magnificent building which was being erected by area craftsmen in just three short months. Oshkosh residents were invited to attend the celebration of the opening in 1903

Photo Credit: Bill Wyman

> *"The people of Oshkosh had convenient transportation to the clubhouse. Trolleys ran from Main Street to Waugoo Street, and Rosalia Street to Washington Boulevard, where it was a block stroll to the clubhouse. For many years, the yacht club grounds proved a mecca for picnickers and observers on weekends. Hundreds of families dotted the clubhouse lawn and lined the two porches of the building to enjoy not only the spectacle of sailboat racing but to socialize as well.*
>
> *Food was served there, dances were danced there, parties were held there and most importantly memories were born there.*
>
> *The building of the clubhouse signaled the beginning of yachting golden's age in Oshkosh."*

Sources: Oshkoshyachtclub.org.; The Centennial Yearbook of the Oshkosh Yacht Club

But that elation and celebration was somewhat short-lived. In 1918, World War I was in full swing and club membership was badly depleted. Unable to make their financial commitments, the clubhouse was sold to the City of Oshkosh where it was used largely for "municipal purposes", but still available to and utilized by the yacht club.

By 1927, the situation started to improve. The war was now behind us and the general outlook became more positive. Memberships at the yacht club burgeoned, and with the help of several donations, the OYC was able to buy back their clubhouse on March 8.

The elation was short-lived once again in 1932. Taxes could not be met and the property was sold to the American Legion, never again to be owned by the Oshkosh Yacht Club. After the American Legion acquired the property, the yacht club was allowed to continue to use it as their headquarters, providing they maintained the harbor and dock areas along the lakefront.

The Legion on the Lake was named so due to the fact it was owned by the Oshkosh American Legion Cook Fuller Post 70 for more than 60 years. I remember attending many occasions there, but my most vivid recollection was the stately manner of the mansion. The main floor was mostly used to setup the band at one end of the vast room. Nearby, a horseshoe shaped bar allowed guests to order their favorite cocktail, listen to the music and dance on a spacious dance floor. Adjacent to the first floor in a delightful location, a large screened porch invited attendees to sit and feel the cool, gentle breeze off the lake. The second story also has a nice dance floor but was not always used. Why not? Because at weddings the beer was usually free and the keg was located in the basement. Guests took trips up and down the stairs to fill pitchers of ice cold Peoples and Chief Oshkosh beer, but no one minded as those trips were well worth the while. Also, it was believed during that time, the present owners were unsure the second floor would withstand the weight of a large group of people. During the recent restoration it was determined the second floor was safe and built to withstand the weight of early day concerns.

In some regards, the stately old mansion felt a little out of place in Oshkosh due to its stature, while on the other hand, it seemed to fit right in at the end of Washington Avenue where many of Oshkosh's premier residences were located. Residents along that corridor were owned by Oshkosh notables, physicians, attorneys and top city officials and business owners.

The Legion was purchased in 2007 by local business family Bill and Beth Wyman (whose family owned and operated Oshkosh B'Gosh for many years). The facility was in need of restoration and many repairs due to years of neglect and non usage. The Wymans made a significant investment to restore the property to its original condition. I asked Bill Wyman about the decision to purchase the property.

"I lived down the street as a little kid and spent many hours playing on the property." Bill reminisced. "We come from a family history of sailing and the Oshkosh Yacht Club needed a home. Sailing and the OYC bring generations of families together in a happy active setting" he continued. "Also, we knew that the Legion was having difficulty managing the property and we did not want to lose a rich part of Oshkosh history."

Now known as *"The Waters"*, (named after the architect William Waters who designed it 105 years earlier), this magnificent Oshkosh landmark once again hosts weddings and special events. The Wyman's have made provisions for the Oshkosh Yacht Club to continue to use a portion of the property as their headquarters, keeping in tradition with the original plan to support yachting and sailing on the shores of Lake Winnebago. The American Legion has a 50 year lease and keeps an office in the lower level. "Twice a month we have 'Legion Night' here at *The Waters*" Bill stated.

Often quietly and without fanfare, the Wymans continue today to give back to the community they love so dearly in so many ways.

The Waters circa 2008
Photo Credit: Randy Domer

Knaggs Ferry

In the early 1800's, James Knaggs operated a ferry to allow travelers passage across the Fox River in Oshkosh. As there were no bridges yet, the Knaggs Ferry was the only way to cross the wide, winding river. Knaggs, the third owner of the ferry, acquired it in 1835. In addition to the ferry, Knaggs also operated a trading post and tavern originally established by George Johnston, then owned by Robert Grignon before being acquired by Knaggs. The business was located on the east side of the Fox River, where Riverside Cemetery is today, but the site of the original buildings is now covered with water.

James Knaggs parentage was recorded to be Potawatomi and Anglo. Originally, permission from the local Menominee Indians to build the trading post and tavern had to be received as it would reside on land owned by the local tribe. (ref. Oshkosh at 150, Michael J. Goc).

James Metz of the Daily Northwestern edited a book titled "Prairie, Pines, and People" published in 1976. In the book Metz and co-author Dr. Charles D. Goff writes *"Knaggs appears to have grown up in Indiana or the Detroit area, and to have come to Green Bay about 1820. He worked for Augustin Grignon's trading enterprise on the Wisconsin River before buying the ferry and tavern."*

Goff also points out *"Knaggs appears to have been defrauded of his ownership of the Algoma Ferry in 1836 by Webster Stanley who worked briefly for Knaggs as a ferryman before taking the ferry downstream to the present Wisconsin-Ohio Street bridge and later to the Yankee settlement at the mouth of the Fox, justifying his actions on the interesting ground that Knaggs was only a half breed."* It continues to say *"James Knaggs, no longer possessing the ferry, became a farmer in the Town of Algoma on West Main Street to the west of the growing settlement"*

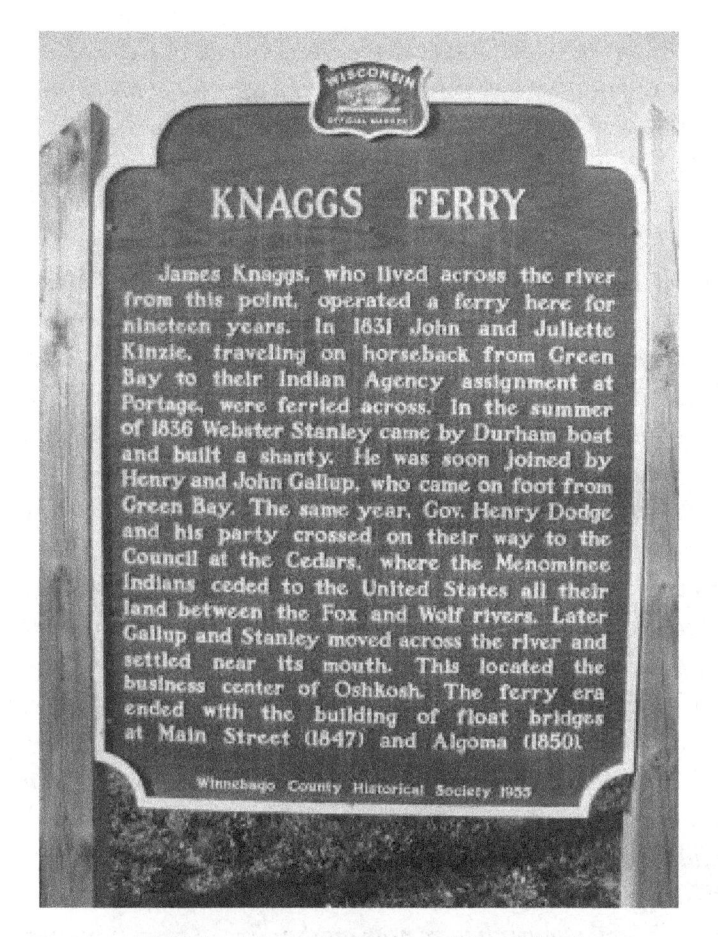

Historical Landmark in Rainbow Park
Photo Credit: Randy Domer

The story of Knaggs life was told by the Oshkosh Northwestern in their April 14, 1948 edition. Here is a transcript of excerpts from that article:

Knaggs Ran Ferry, Trading Post for Travelers over Century Ago

"One of the men who left an imprint on history in Oshkosh that cannot easily be overlooked was an Indian half-breed by the name of James Knaggs. Sometimes described as the city's first merchant, and the operator of the first ferry service…"

"Knaggs operated his combined trading post, general store, and restaurant in a log cabin where Riverside Cemetery is now located. The business *was started on the opposite side of the river, known as Coon's Point (Rainbow Park today), but was soon moved to the east side of the river. This was in the year 1836, a dozen years before Wisconsin's statehood..."*

"Knaggs immediately opened his trading post, which handled a large stock of Indian goods. The late W.W. Wright, third permanent white settler in Oshkosh, said that Knaggs came from Indiana. He was a half-breed Pottawatomi. He married a Menominee squaw..."

"FLEETER THAN A HORSE: It was James Jr. who carried the mail for several years from Green Bay to Fort Winnebago on foot. 'I was told he could make better time on foot than he could with an Indian pony,' Wright wrote. Oshkosh settlers were required to go to Green Bay to receive their mail in those days, because there was no post office here..."

"The elder Knaggs himself was a tough, wiry man. Of him also it was said that he could out travel a horse with a man on his back. The half-breed was a noted character among the Indians and many half-breeds that had moved to his vicinity, and was looked up to as sort of leader among them, Wright pointed out..."

"Knaggs residence was a double log shanty where he would keep travelers overnight 'and always furnish them with drinks at 25 cents a glass with meals $1 and nothing to brag of at that' Wright declared. 'But travelers did not stop at trifles in those days and were glad to get what they could and be thankful for that', he explained..."

"Knaggs did little farming, but lived by his ferrying and trade with the Indians. Several wigwams were near his dwelling. Other Indians passed up and down the river constantly, always stopping at Knaggs' landing and selling their furs or whatever they might have to barter..."

"Knaggs ferryboat was a flat bottomed scow, large enough to transport horses across the river..."

"Probably just an interesting a yarn as Knaggs, is the story of Mrs. John Kinzie, a well-known educated, refined woman of Chicago, who once paid for an overnight visit to Knaggs 'Hotel'. In her autobiography of 'Wau-Bun – The Early Days in the Northwest', Mrs. Kinzie provided a vivid account of the visit to Knaggs' landing on a journey with her husband on horseback from Fort Howard to Fort Winnebago...She won the distinction of having been the first white woman to pass through this territory and the first to make the journey between two government forts, sleeping one night at Knaggs' post in a one-room building which the party was compelled to share with a snoring Indian..."

"ATE, VENISON, BEAR MEAT: 'As we had only broken our fast since morning with a few crackers we carried in our pockets. We did ample justice to her nice coffee and cakes, not to mention venison steaks and bear's meat, the latter of which I had never before tasted' Mrs. Kinzie declared. After eating, the Kinzies inquired about a place to sleep". Kinzie writes 'We took a look at it. It consisted of one room, bare and dirty. Against one chimney was built a rickety sort of bunk. This was the only vestige of furniture to be seen. The floor was thickly covered with mud, and a weak fire burned in another chimney. There was no alternative. The only thing Mr. Knaggs could furnish in the way of bedding was a small bearskin. The bunk was a trifle less filthy than the floor, so upon the boards we spread first the skin, then our saddle blankets, and with a pair of saddlebags for a bolster (pillow), I wrapped myself in my cloak and resigned myself to the distasteful accommodations...it was relief to rise with early morning and prepare for the journey of the day'..."

Lantern Tree
Photo Credit: Randy Domer

Today, the site of the ferry is marked by two landmarks. On the west bank, a historical marker stands along the banks of the river in what is now Rainbow Park (formerly Coon's Point). Across the way, on the east side of river, the landing is quietly and discreetly marked by "The Old Lantern Tree". Legend tells us Knaggs placed a lantern in a tree to mark the landing site on that side of the river. Believe it or not, the tree, although petrified, still stands there today! It is located in today's Riverside cemetery. As the marker testifies, the ferry era in Oshkosh came to an end in 1847 when the first float bridge was erected at Main Street and then in 1850 on Algoma.

Some of the descendents to James Knaggs still reside in Oshkosh today. One of these descendents, Neil Knaggs, is married to my sister-in-law Lois (née Steinert). Neil has two brothers, Charles and James, and three sons and one daughter.

James has one daughter and one son. All three Knaggs brothers, sons of Clifford and Leona Knaggs, reside in Oshkosh today.

Oshkosh's Very Own...

RICHARD "TICKER" REICHENBERGER

It began in the era when Oshkosh, like most other cities, was abundant with corner grocery stores. Commonly called "Mom and Pop" stores, the name meant the stores were usually owned and operated by a man and his wife and in many cases, the entire family. The 1960's started signaling the end of the corner grocery store. This was a time before "supermarkets" came into existence and one by one, slowly pushed the small merchants right out of business.

Reichenbergers was one of the most popular little grocery stores in town was located on the corner of Sixth Ave and Knapp Street, across the street from Sacred Heart Church. The Reichenberger family built their reputation on custom cut quality fresh meats and homemade sausages. It was here that "Ticker" Reichenberger found his calling in the meat business. Perhaps one of the best known people in the Oshkosh area, Ticker's name became synonymous with "good meat".

Ticker recalls "The store was originally built by my dad's dad around 1915. Then after World War I, my dad came home and started running the business a couple of years later". Ticker is one of six children of Ferdinand (Fernie) and Ann Reichenberger. In 1933, Richard John Reichenberger was born at home, above the store where the family lived and ran their grocery business.

Ticker related that he didn't start working in the store until he was 18 years old. Other than the few menial chores most boys his age had back then, Ticker said his dad didn't believe in kids working at such a young age. "My dad told me '*It was a time in life when kids should be playing*', he said. Ticker followed in his brother's footsteps as brothers Ralph, Vern and Joe took up the knife and saw in the family business.

"I learned to cut meat from my dad!" he proudly grinned. "My dad was a hell of a meat cutter. He could turn a $1 roast into a $2 roast!" he said with a laugh.

Ticker married his boyhood sweetie Susie in 1957. They have five children all born within five years of each other. I asked Ticker how he and Susie met. He chuckled and said "Well, she used to come in the store all the time...we were about 12 I think. Then I used to throw snowballs at her!" he said as he sat back in his chair with a hearty laugh.

Ticker, an athlete in his own right, played baseball, basketball and football in high school. "Baseball and softball were my favorite" he said. After high school, he recalls playing softball and one season his team, Mueller Shell, won the State Championship.

He liked playing the outfield and Herb Tesch, one of Ticker's teammates pointed out that Reichenberger "was a hell of a drag bunter too!"

Richard "Ticker" Reichenberger
Photo Credit: Randy Domer

Ticker loves to talk with people and has a dozen stories at the ready. Just about any topic mentioned to him, will trigger his memory and then he begins to spin his tales. My favorite story is one he shared with me when we were working together. "Our family store was right across the street from Sacred Heart Church. And every week, the Sisters from the church would walk over and do their weekly grocery shopping. In those days, the Sisters had no transportation so the store was a huge convenience. If they wanted to go downtown, they took the city bus. One day, my dad decided he wanted to buy a car and donate it to them. It was a station wagon. And you know what Randy?" (Here he pauses, looks around as if to see if anyone else was in earshot... then finishes...) "After that, we never saw them!" (He breaks out with his trademark laugh here). "Now that they had wheels, they shopped somewhere else!" he said as he continued laughing.

Ticker reminisced about the World War II era and reminded me that meat rationing was a big deal. Tuesdays became "Meatless Tuesday" and people had stamps and tokens to buy meat on the other days. "Besides that…we closed on Sunday. All stores were closed on Sunday back then. It's a wonder we could even make it in the business".

I've known and worked with Ticker for many years. Our conversation this day was relaxed and one of two friends, sharing a Coke and reminiscing. As the conversation started to wane, I set down my pen and asked "Ticker…what would you say you are most proud of in your life?" He didn't say anything for what seemed forever. Finally, he said quietly as he folded his hands, looking down at the table. "You know Randy; I well up every time I think of it…it was my Dad. It was coming to the realization that my Dad was the best man I ever knew." Tears came to his eyes and he took a moment to compose himself. "Let me tell you what I mean. Quite a few years ago, a man approached me; a man I had not known or previously met. He introduced himself and proceeded to tell me a story. The man said he had decided to leave Oshkosh to pursue new interests. Upon leaving, his father said to him *"When, or if you ever come back to Oshkosh, you grab a phonebook. If you see the name Reichenberger in it, I want you to give all your business to that name. If it wasn't for Fernie Reichenberger, we wouldn't be here today"* Ticker then paused a moment to again collect himself. "You see, during that era things were tough with the depression and all. I didn't find out until later years that my Dad would forgive debt to neighbors and friends who didn't have the means to pay their bill. That's the kind of man my father was! It was a time when people looked out for each other."

In 1978, the doors to Reichenbergers closed for the last time.

Ticker Reichenberger is a man that I am proud to call my friend. We've stood shoulder to shoulder at the butcher block, flashed steel and shared dozens of stories over the years. Today Ticker is closing in on 80 years young. He works four days a week at Festival Foods and the other three days helping his son Kevin in his Reichenberger Meats business. He is one of the most well known figures in the city of Oshkosh and recognizes just about everyone that pushes a grocery cart past his work station. Always quick with a joke, anecdote or helpful cooking tip, Ticker greets everyone he meets eagerly and with a smile. Does he have plans to retire? When I asked him that question, he got a twinkle in his eye, and then said, "I wake up every morning ready to go! I love the people part of this business…that's what it's all about!"

Little Oscar stops at Reichenbergers while passing through Oshkosh in his Oscar Mayer Wienermobile. Posing with the "World's Smallest Chef"   Left to Right - Frank "Reggie" Reichenberger, Ticker Reichenberger, L'il Oscar and Fernie Reichenberger

Photo Credit Dan Radig

Trail's End

Most often, we think of historic landmarks in Oshkosh as old hotels, opera houses or stately mansions like the Public Museum, Paine Art Center or The Waters.

On the northeast corner of Broad Street and Merritt sits a corner tavern that built its fame and fortune around nothing less than… a hot dog!

If you lived in Oshkosh at anytime in the twentieth century, you knew about these "world famous" treasures. Records indicate the tavern was built as early as the 1887, and has passed through various ownerships through the years. Today, Trail's End is owned and operated by Bob Winkleman, who bought the business in April of 1985 from John Abraham and Edward John.

My memories go back to the 1950's when the tavern was owned by Bill Vandenberg. Known then as "Van's", hot dogs were only a dime, or ten for a buck then! My dad would drive all the way across town, grab a bag of "Van's" dogs and feed the entire family for a dollar!

According to Winkleman, Vandenberg started selling hot dogs in 1926. "Van got the recipe for his hot dogs from a restaurant on Main Street that was going out of business" Bob shared with me. And here is where the conversation gets interesting. "The secret is in the sauce. I'd be a rich man if I had a dime for everyone that asked me for the recipe over the years" he grinned. "But it's a well guarded secret. Every once in awhile, someone will stop in and say they have the recipe, but it doesn't quite taste like yours". To which Bob always responds with "…well, I guess you don't have the original recipe then, do you?"

If you've never had a Trail's End Hot Dog, let me describe how this masterpiece is made. First, you take a quality wiener that is purchased locally. No secret here, it's a german style wiener from a recipe developed by Bob Meyer of Meyer's Sausage in Oshkosh, but now produced by Silver Creek. Put it in a fresh, steamed bun, cover the wiener with heaping spoonfuls of "secret sauce", and then smother it with as many fresh chopped onions as you can! According to Winkelman, the original recipe was changed slightly over the years. "When I bought the place, I discovered previous owners had tweaked the original recipe. I sat down with Pep, a long time Trail's End bartender and we put things back to the original way", he said.

Clarence Steinhilber was that bartender and tended bar for many years at Trail's End and was well known by local patrons for decades. Known as "Pep" by the regular customers, Steinhilber started calling on "Van's" when he was 16 years old. "He sold chickens to Vandenberg" Bob claims. "Eventually he went to work for Van and moved behind the bar." Pep continued to work with each new owner as the business was sold multiple times. Winkleman recalls, "Pep was a great guy. You never heard him say a bad word about anyone". Today, behind the bar, stands a hand painted picture of "Pep" done by his grandson. It is placed there to honor his memory with all the people he served for so many years.

Trail's End 1966
Photo Credit: Dan Radig, FB

Van's and Trail's End hot dog's reputation was famous beyond our city limits. Bob also shared a story that, years ago, when passenger trains regularly stopped in Oshkosh, they would call ahead and place an order for hot dogs. When the train would pull into the depot located just across the street and a block down, the conductor would walk over and pickup the order!

Winkleman remembers one of the previous owners having a pet parrot behind the bar. "He had excellent language skills", Bob laughed, as he told me how the bird would entertain customers. I'll let your imagination decide what a parrot who lived in a tavern might say...

Today, its estimated Trail's End sells about 1200 dogs per week in winter and about 1700 per week during the summer months. The bar and back bar are original. The booths that used to line the walls of the dining area are still intact and stored back in a closed in storage area. A pool table and wall now replace the area where patrons would come in, slide into a booth and ring the buzzer on the wall when they were ready to order their perch or chicken dinner. The kitchen area then was located at the north end of building behind two western style swinging doors.

Today, the food menu is just sandwiches and pizza. But not just any sandwich...besides their trademark hot dogs, you can order a braunschweiger or brick cheese sandwich. Order the combo to get a little of both. Hot dogs are no longer a dime but obviously a big seller at $1.85 each or 3 for $5.

The building is well maintained but showing her age. "She leans a little bit, but wouldn't you too if you were standing for over 100 years!" Bob jokes.

You can find some pretty good hot dogs around town. The Magnet was always very famous for their dogs, but to most long time residents, Trail's End is number one.

The original sign still stands behind the bar promoting "World Famous" hot dogs. And they are just that.

Sawyer Street Ball Diamond

One of my fondest memories was lying on my parents' bed on a hot summer evening, listening to Blaine Walsh and Earl Gillespie calling the Milwaukee Braves game, and looking out the window at the lights glaring from the ball field on Sawyer Street.

It was a grand place where my boyhood dreams of someday being in the big leagues played out. The ballpark seemed enormous to me at about 8 or 9 years old. Local teams, the Oshkosh Giants or the American Legion, offered promising prospects the opportunity to hone their skills.

Herb Willis, sports director and announcer from local radio station WOSH was always there and seemed to me to be the guy running the show. Herb would drive into the gravel parking lot along the north side of the field in his WOSH station wagon, get into his wheelchair, and then make his way toward the field. Herb would offer us 25 cents per ball to shag and return foul balls. It was quite a scramble to beat the neighborhood kids for those balls. Some of the older and faster boys did better, but strategy would come into play. Not only did I have to get to the ball first, I had to out run the other kids to get the ball to Herb before they caught me and took the ball away!

Occasionally, we would sit across the street to the west, directly behind the backstop and in the driveway of the Standard Oil Station. The "filling station" was usually closed in the evenings, so we would park our bikes, kickstand down, and sit and wait for a foul ball to come over the backstop. The ball would come flying over the backstop at lightning speed and usually hit Sawyer Street on the first bounce. Then the idea was to grab it on the way down, jump on your bike and head for the hills. Our bikes would spit gravel as we tore through the gravel parking lot of The Club tavern located just across the street. That is also how we would get the balls needed to play in our neighborhood field lots. We would use those balls until the cover starting coming off, then take a roll of electrical tape from my dad's garage, tape it up and continue using it. Occasionally, we would score a broken Louisville Slugger bat from one of the teams. We would take the bat home and find a screw and tape to hold it together. When it got hot, that electrical tape would get so sticky it was better than today's pine tar. And if you hit the ball just so, the vibration would sting your hands like they fell asleep!

But the Sawyer Street ball field was a beauty in and of itself. The infield was lined with chain link fence. A backstop provided protection to fans seated on the wood plank grandstand bleachers that wrapped around the infield from first to third base. Directly behind home plate was the "press box". Below, a concrete block concession stand sold peanuts, popcorn, crackerjack, hotdogs, soda and beer.

The outfield was lined with green boards arranged vertically. The scoreboard was located in right-center field. Marked with "Home" and "Visitors", it was far from high tech. The "scorer" would walk along a wood plank suspended under the scoreboard, and hang the numbers on hooks each time a team would score. The dugouts were made of wood. The weathered worn, creaky plank benches covered with cleat marks were the evidence of the likes of Dave Garcia, Hank Bauer and major league hopefuls and prospects that sat here, looking out over their very own "Field of Dreams" imagining what it would be like to make "The Biggies".

Sawyer Street Ball Field, circa 1950's
Photo Credit: Ed and August Tiedje

Oshkosh's Very Own...

SPORTS HEROES

If you're from Oshkosh, you already know about some of the home-grown talents that were born and raised right here. Names like Billy Hoeft, Howie Koplitz, Dave Tyriver, Bill Gogolewski and Dutch Rennert top the bill for those who made it to baseball's major leagues.

I had the good fortune to know or at least meet most of these men through various circumstances. And each and every one of them was the most congenial and gracious to talk with. Always willing to answer questions and share a yarn or two about their experiences, and always with a high degree of modesty.

I had the good fortune to play slow pitch softball in the mid 1970's with Dave Tyriver, Howie Koplitz and Roger LaPoint. The team was First English Lutheran and competed in the Thursday Night League at Sawyer Street's Southside Lighted Diamond located on South Sawyer at the end of Seventh Avenue. It was a very competitive league with teams like Red's Pizza and Jackie's Beauty's. Many of these teams were made of players from the classic league, a very talented bunch of fence busters as I recall from my pitching days. Dave and Howie had MLB playing experience...Dave with the Indians and Howie with the Tigers and Senators.

First English Lutheran Softball Team 1975. Standing: Jeff Koplitz, Dave Tyriver, Rev. Roald Harswick, Terry Seaborn, Bill Green, Roger LaPoint, Howie Koplitz   Bottom Row: Rob Schneider, Randy Domer, Mark Harswick, Tim Westenberger, Darryl Kumbier, Dick Schammens

Photo taken at the Southside Lighted Diamond on Sawyer St.

Oshkosh's Very Own...
Dave Tyriver

Dave Tyriver was a professional baseball player in many respects. He had excellent speed and an arm that earned him the coveted center fielder position on the First English Lutheran softball team. His arm was like a cannon and on more than one occasion, I saw Dave fire a bullet from center field and throw a runner out at home trying to stretch his luck. Dave was someone I admired and liked because he always had a smile on his face and would always ask how you were doing or offer a tip or two on your play. When I knew Dave, his major league days were behind him, but you wouldn't know it by looking at him. He took very good care of himself physically. In those days, Dave worked at Rohner's Furniture on Oregon Street. Born on Sunday, October 31, 1937 in Oshkosh Wisconsin, Tyriver was 24 years old when he broke into the majors on August 21, 1962, with the Cleveland Indians. Originally signed by Cleveland as an Amateur Free Agent, his contract was purchased by the Senators in October of 1961.

By the following April, he was returned to the Indians as part of a conditional deal. Dave was a right handed pitcher and threw four games for the Tribe in his brief MLB career. His stats for the 4 games he appeared in are: 4.92 ERA, pitched 10.2 innings giving up 10 hits and 5 earned runs, 2 HR's, 7 BB's and 7 SO's. He also had 3 AB's striking out twice.

Dave Tyriver with the Cleveland Indians
Photo Credit: Herb Tesch

Sadly, we lost Dave at a very early age in life. He passed away on October 28, 1988, just 3 days short of his 51st birthday.

Oshkosh's Very Own...
Howie Koplitz

Howie Koplitz was the silent leader on our First English Lutheran Church softball team. He showed up every week, warmed up and took his place in the infield. Not a lot of chatter but prodded teammates when the situation called for it. He played a flawless second base and batted third in our lineup, right before Tyriver. Howie and Dave gave us the one-two punch we needed by driving in runs and getting on base.

Howie was born on May 4, 1938 and pitched five years in the majors for Detroit and Washington. His first major league appearance was with the Tigers on September 8, 1961. That year, the Tigers won 101 games, but were edged from post season play by the Yankees who finished 8 games ahead of them.

During his 5 year career, Howie went 9-7 and earned an era of 4.21 with 87 strikeouts. Koplitz notched his first major league win with Detroit on September 24, 1961 with a 7-5 victory over the Los Angeles Angels. Howie went on to win his next 6 decisions and was 7-0 when an arm injury sidelined his career. While in the minors, Howie tossed a no hitter and an outstanding pitching record of 23-3 with the Tigers AA club Birmingham. In 1961, Koplitz was named Minor League Player of the Year.

Howie Koplitz with the Washington Senators
Photo Credit: Herb Tesch

During his career, Howie had the honor to play with notable greats such as Al Kaline, Norm Cash, Rocky Colavito, Mgr Gil Hodges, Don Zimmer and Frank Howard.

After his major league career, Howie returned home to Oshkosh and was deeply involved with local sports teams and organizations. He is a former director of *The Snitz Club,* an Oshkosh group of people dedicated to supporting baseball in Oshkosh. Howie also coached baseball at Lourdes High School.

Recently, I opened up the morning newspaper and was saddened to see that on January 2, 2012, Howie Koplitz passed away at age 73.

Oshkosh's Very Own...
Bill Gogolewski

In 1969, I joined the Wisconsin National Guard's 1157 Transportation Company located at the end of Armory Place off Ninth St. It was there I had the chance to meet Bill Gogolewski. "Gogo" was a right handed pitcher drafted out of high school by the Washington Senators in June of 1965 in the MLB's first ever Amateur Draft. Bill worked in the minors for five seasons before being called up late in 1968, then in August 1970 when Bill found a spot on the Senators roster. That month he started 5 of 8 games winning two of four decisions. In 1971, the Senators last year in Washington, Bill went 6-5 in 17 outings and a "sweet" 2.76 ERA. The Senators then moved to Texas where Gogo pitched until his trade to Cleveland came in March 1974. Released by the Indians in 1975, Bill immediately was signed by the Chicago White Sox. It was that season the long, lanky right-hander's MLB career came to an end due to an elbow injury.

Bill "Gogo" Gogolewski as a Washington Senator
Photo Credit: Herb Tesch

Like his Oshkosh predecessors, Bill had the honor of playing with some of baseball's big icons like Denny McClain, Curt Flood, Mgr Ted Williams, Coach Nellie Fox, Mgr Billy Martin, Mgr Whitey Herzog, Gaylord Perry, Frank Robinson, Frank Howard and Goose Gossage to name a few.

I met Bill for breakfast one morning and as he strolled into "Two Brothers" restaurant on the west side of town. He looked to me like he could still bring the heat as we shook hands, grabbed a cup of coffee and began to talk baseball.

I asked Bill about the toughest batter that he faced in his career. "Rod Carew" he replied without hesitation. "He was one of the best contact hitters in baseball." As we continued our talk, I reminded Bill he had played for two pretty tough managers in his career...Ted Williams and Billy Martin. So, who was the hardest to play under? "Both men had their different styles", Gogo replied. "Ted Williams managed like he played, always looking for the big inning". He thought a moment then continued, "Billy Martin played 'Billy Ball,' which meant a lot of action, bunting, stealing anything you could do to advance the runner and score runs". When I asked him about anything memorable that stood out in his career, he laughed and said "Yeah, the time Denny McClain stepped on my ankle and put me on the disabled list!"

Bill is a tall and slender, and looks exactly like what a major league pitcher should look like. One day at our National Guard summer camp at Fort McCoy, Gogo flipped me a glove and said "set up down there and I'll toss you a few". I took the glove and assumed my best catchers position. Gogo tossed a few warm-ups, and then decided to surprise me with a fastball. The ball went whizzing by me before I could even move my glove to catch it! I walked out into the field, retrieved the ball and tossed it back to him. I then told Bill I was going to situate myself against one of the barracks, using it as a backstop in the likely event I miss another one. Bill took a full windup and fired another fastball, this time it went sailing past my ear and hit the side of building. The old 1940's shingles covering the building shattered like broken glass. I stood up, looked at him and he was grinning from ear to ear. I laid my glove back on the ground and said "You're crazy!" We both had a good laugh and I became friends with Bill after that. In later years, I moved away from Oshkosh and attended a Major League Baseball Alumni golf outing in Lake Geneva, Wisconsin. Gogo was there as one of the retired players and he arranged for us to golf together. That was a very memorable day for me.

Oshkosh's Very Own...
"Dutch" Rennert

S-s-s-s-t-t-t-e-e-e-r-i-k-e Three! Yer out! (Fist pump) This famous call was the trademark of Oshkosh's Dutch Rennert, a 20 year veteran as a National League Umpire. Dutch's umpiring style made him both famous and popular throughout the league and fan base alike.

Born Laurence Henry Rennert, in Oshkosh on June 12, 1930, the cigar smoking man-in-blue's interest in baseball started at an early age. In high school, Dutch played on the Oshkosh Indians High School and American Legion Baseball teams with future major leaguer Billy Hoeft and a host of other very talented ballplayers. In fact, the 1947 Legion team that year won the regional, sectional and State title in the Wisconsin State League.

1947 Oshkosh Legion Team
Photo Credit: Herb Tesch

*Top row: L. Bartelt (coach), T. Poeschl, B. Zarling, J. Drexler,
L. Nickels, B. Hoeft, D. Weed, C. Hecker (coach)
Bottom row: L. "Dutch" Rennert, W. Reque, G. Mohr, H. Tesch,
B. Fenrich, G. Brewer, K. Mueller*

    I had the opportunity to speak with Dutch recently; in fact it was just one month shy of his 82nd birthday. Dutch and his wife Shirley have retired, and now make their home in Vero Beach Florida.

    As we began to chat, I soon realized baseball was not Dutch's only interest in sports. He played quarterback for the high school team under Coach Harold Schumerth. "I only weighed 160 pounds then" he said. Then his quick wit and sense of humor kicked in "…I played quarterback because you had have brains to play back there!" He said it was one of his most cherished memories in his life. "We won the championship in 1949. It was the first championship in the history of OHS, before the expansion of the Fox Valley Conference. What made it extra special was it was Coach Schumerth's first championship since he started coaching in 1940…I'll never forget that".

During his high school years, Dutch played centerfield under Coach EJ Schneider. "I was all field and no hit", quipped Rennert. "You could shake an apple tree and get a hundred outfielders, but you've got to be able to hit. I couldn't hit the curveball." He then explained, "It wasn't until I got into umpiring to understand why. I wasn't watching the ball all the way to the plate."

When he talks about high school teammate Billy Hoeft, he has nothing but high praise for the Oshkosh southpaw. "He was the best pitcher I'd ever seen play in high school", he said. "Between high school and the American Legion years, Hoeft won 37 games in a row!" Dutch went on to say, "I was on the Oshkosh City Cabs team when we beat Billy and broke his 37 game win streak. It was an exhibition game over at the Sawyer Street ball diamond." Without missing a beat, Dutch continued his story. "It was probably the seventh inning. I got on base and stole second. Then player/manager Herm Schumacher hit a triple and we beat them 3-2…that was Billy's first defeat in 38 games."

"The Oshkosh City Cabs was a good team too" Dutch explained. "Guys like Richie Lautenschlager and Gordy Tellock…all good ball players".

After high school, Dutch played some semi pro football for the Oshkosh Comets and started doing a little umpiring. "In 1956, we went out to Las Vegas to see about doing some basketball promotions with Abe Saperstein, who managed promotions for traveling teams like the Harlem Globetrotters, the New York Renaissance, the professional woman's team the All American Red Heads, etc. While in Las Vegas, Dutch was having dinner one evening with Marques Haynes of the Harlem Globetrotters. Haynes also worked with the local Rec Department in Vegas at the time and was looking for some assistance finding umpires. Dutch remembers "Haynes asked if I'd ever thought about umpiring. He said 'we pay $10 per game, two games a night, and we furnish the equipment'. I was looking for a way to make some money and thought what the heck?" Rennert worked all summer long that year umpiring in the Las Vegas Recreational League.

It was several months later that season, Dutch heard a knock at the umpire's room door at Recreation Park. "I opened the door and there stood a tall grey haired gentleman. He introduced himself as Joe Rue, retired American League umpire and asked me if I had a minute. I said sure, invited him in and we sat down." Rue then went on to explain he had been watching Dutch work in the Rec League. "I've been watching you all summer long, and it's evident you don't know all the rules. But for a guy with no formal training, you seem to have a lot of natural ability. Have you ever thought of going to Umpire School?" Rue asked.

Dutch thought for a minute and then to himself said, "*Heck, who would ever want to be an umpire?*"

As time passed, Dutch gave more thought to opportunity. The following spring, February 1957, he decided to join Umpire School. The school was located in Daytona Beach and run by a friend of Joe Rue who was good enough to give Dutch a recommendation. After finishing school, Dutch began working the "D" League in Alabama.

For the next 16 years, Dutch worked his way through the minor leagues advancing his status and experience along the way. This tenure is unheard of today. "For a promising umpire to spend 16 years toiling away in the minors is something you won't find today. You see, back then, we only had one supervisor that covered maybe 40 leagues nationally. You seldom if ever saw a supervisor, or did the supervisor personally ever see you work. You gained your reputation by what GM's, Managers and players said about you. That was tough you know…if you made a tough call that went against a team, you think the manager or player is going to say good things about you?" Dutch explained. Today Rennert estimates there are 10-12 supervisors in the leagues.

A little known highlight of his career came one day in Macon Georgia. Dutch was working in the Southern Association and was on the field when Oshkosh native Howie Koplitz threw his no-hitter. Koplitz was pitching for the Birmingham Barons, a Detroit Tigers AA farm team. Dutch had first base that day. "What a thrill to see a fellow from your hometown throw a no-hitter…I'll never forget it"

In the early 1970's, Dutch finally got his break. "Al Barlick, a 32 year veteran, decided to retire and the league put him in charge of umpires. Immediately Barlick said we need to staff the majors with people of experience" Dutch offered. "Previous to that, in the American League they were hiring former football players like Hank Soar, Bill Kinnamon, Charlie Berry, and Cal Hubbard…big guys. They were hiring by size, not experience." He continued "The National League was hiring guys like Augie Donatelli, Jocko Conlan, Shag Crawford, Stan Landes and the sort." Dutch credits Al Barlick with bringing him into the majors. "If it wasn't for Al Barlick, I wouldn't be where I am today."

In 1971, MLB picked up the options on Dutch's contract but placed him back in the minor leagues as there were no openings yet in the big leagues.

Rennert finally broke into the "bigs" in 1973 at Montreal with the Expo's hosting the New York Mets. That evening, Tom Seaver was on the mound for the Mets. "I walked out onto the field, looked around and said to myself *I made it! After 16 years in the minors, I finally made it!! They can never take this moment away from me.*" He then explained how his thoughts changed direction to the importance of his new status. "You can miss a call in Amarillo Texas and it's no big deal. But when you're in New York and miss a call, the whole world knows about it the next day with all the media coverage."

That evening, Dutch called home and talked with his wife. "I was looking out my hotel room window, gazing at the Montreal skyline and told her… *well, I'm in the record books now*" he said with pride. "*They can never take that away from me.*" Today, as he reflects back on his storied career, he still has that sense of pride and accomplishment.

Through the 20 years he spent working Major League Baseball, Dutch has earned so many great highlights and experiences along the way. I asked him to share a few with me.

"The three World Series games were probably my proudest moments" he shared. "It was the 1989 Series between the Oakland Athletics and the San Francisco Giants at Candlestick Park. About five minutes before the game was due to start, the whole place started shaking! We were right in the middle of an earthquake!" In addition to the memorable '89 Series, Dutch also umpired the 1980 (Kansas City Royals vs Philadelphia Phillies) and 1983 World Series (Baltimore Orioles vs Philadelphia Phillies).

Who was the toughest manager to face on the field? "Lou Piniella, without a doubt. The first thing he would do as he came out of the dugout was to throw his hat. That's an automatic ejection right there! He hasn't even had the chance to argue the call, and he's gone! He had a short fuse…" he said. He then continued "One day, Lou threw two bases at me! I was calling first base and just made a double play call that went against him. He got so worked up, he pulled the bases right out of the ground and threw them. Naturally, that one still plays out on a lot of highlight reels even today"

Dutch named the three best managers in baseball in that era. "Walter Alston of the LA Dodgers was a gentleman. He didn't come out on the field ranting and raving. He'd walk over to you and discuss the call." Without pause he went to say "Whitey Herzog and Jim Leyland were among the best in baseball…and Leyland is still skipper today in Detroit. All three were strict managers and they didn't take any guff from the players. The players respected them."

Having worked the "speaker circuit" during the offseason, Dutch had numerous anecdotes to share. "I was behind the plate in Pittsburgh one night. Richie Zisk, the Pirates' outfielder was having one of the worst nights of his career with the bat. I called him out on strikes twice and the third time he went down swinging. Fourth time up, he strikes out again! As he walked away from home plate he mumbled something. I took off my mask and said to him *Richie, did you say something?* To which he turned and replied *Why don't you guess…you've been guessing all night."*

Dutch beamed with pride as he talked about being on the field during the game when Pete Rose got his 4000th hit. "If you can imagine the moment, 65,000 fans standing with a 20 minute ovation…what a thrill…it was really something." He then went on to say how bad he feels for Rose's ban from baseball. "You know gambling is just not tolerated in the major leagues. It's the kiss of death. There are signs posted all over, in the clubhouse, everywhere warning personnel about the penalty for gambling. It's too bad though, he was such a talented player."

Finally, I got around to the question I had been waiting ask. How did you get the name "Dutch"? He laughed and said "I went to a Catholic School in Oshkosh…St Joseph's. On the playground the kids came up with the name because it

Dutch Rennert

Photo Credit: Herb Tesch

sounded like the Cubs knuckleball pitcher Dutch Leonard. The Cubbies were the favorite team back then because remember the Braves were not in Milwaukee yet."

I had the honor to meet Dutch one day when he was home during the off season. Dutch and his wife Shirley lived one block away from my boyhood home on Lark Street. It was July 4th, 1981 in the morning when I was working as a meat cutter at the Supervalu store on Sawyer Street, right behind Dutch's house. A call came into the meat department and it was Shirley Rennert, Dutch's wife. Shirley wanted to make a rump roast for their holiday dinner and called to place a "special order". She asked when she could pick it up when I told her I was getting ready to leave and would drop it off on my way home. She was delighted and agreed.

I went into the cooler and selected the nicest rump roast I could find. After weighing it, I wrapped it up nicely in white butcher paper, took off my apron, punched out, went through the check stand to pay for the roast and headed for my car. Moments later I arrived at Dutch's house. I pulled into the driveway, walked to the side door and rang the bell. Shirley came to the door and invited me in. Dutch came into the kitchen, brandishing his trademark unlit cigar clenched in his teeth, and shook my hand while introducing himself. I told Dutch he needed no introduction with me. He invited me to sit down at the kitchen table and offered me a cup of coffee. We sat and talked baseball and I was in awe. Here was a guy that took the field with so many of my baseball heroes. I asked many questions and he never hesitated to tell me stories of his incredible MLB experiences. Dutch became a very popular public speaker telling many of these stories as a profession after he retired from baseball. I knew it was time for me to get going as it was Sunday and my family was waiting for me to come home, so I stood up and shook Dutch's hand once again, thanking him for taking time to visit with me. Dutch stood up, unlit cigar still clenched in his teeth, and said "Wait right here". A minute later he came back into the room clutching two baseballs. He handed it to me and said "Here, thought you might like this." It was a 1976 Phillies Team ball autographed by the entire team. I took the ball, turned it around as I admired the signatures of Mike Schmidt, Steve Carlton, Larry Bowa and others. He then took another ball, autographed it, and handed to me. I stuffed the balls into my coat pocket, reached out and shook his hand one more time and said "Thanks Dutch"! Shirley paid me for the roast and thanked me, reminding me that's really why I was here. I still have the balls encased in plastic sitting on a shelf in my home today.

During his 20 year major league career, Dutch umpired in seven playoff games, two All Star Games and three World Series.

Oshkosh's Very Own...
Herb Tesch

I met Herb Tesch during my tenure in the National Guard and it was there we became good friends. In fact, Herb contributed some of the anecdotes and photos included in this chapter.

I called "Herbie" just recently and he informed me that he recently celebrated his 82nd birthday.

Herb was an athlete in his own right as a young man. Graduating from High School in 1950, Herb excelled in several sports but especially baseball, basketball and football. He was teammates with Dutch Rennert and Billy Hoeft in both baseball and basketball. Additionally, Herb played on the Oshkosh Giants and Oshkosh Legion baseball teams and was a standout outfielder in high school.

In 1951 he played on the City AAA Basketball Team with Dutch Rennert and Billy Hoeft.

Herb also played semi pro baseball with the Ripon Robins. Herb recalled, "I decided to play with them right after high school. The main reason I did was because they picked me up and took me back home after each game. Besides that, they paid me!" Herb had size on his side and had good pro potential until an arm injury while playing with the Giants ended his aspirations. Herb loves sports. He refereed basketball and football and umpired baseball for 9 years in the UW system. A little known fact is that Herb holds a record that he is proud of even until this day. As a kicker for his high school team The Oshkosh Indians and then the semi-pro team Oshkosh Comets, Herb never missed a single extra point or field goal. In the 1949 championship season for the Oshkosh Indians, class mate and friend Dutch Rennert remembered

SPORTS HEROES

1951 City AAA Basketball Team
Top Row: D. Rennert (mgr), R. Nord, H Teteak, D. Biebel,
B. Robien, P. Tesch
Bottom Row: B. Hoeft, D. Popp, C. Erban, J. Peterson,
H. Tesch, L. Gauger, J. Vandershee

Photo Credit: Herb Tesch

1955 Oshkosh Giants (Fox Valley League)
Photo Credit: Herb Tesch

Top Row: R. Borst, D. Teteak, K. Putzer, L. Gauger, W. Reque,
J. Retzloff, B. Peters, H. Tesch, C. Hecker
Bottom Row: G. Mohr, J. Zelmer, B. Koss, P. Tesch, K. Mueller,
M. Peters, C. Peters

Herb kicking the winning field goal, beating Appleton 17-14 over on Jackson Drive at the athletic field.

He worked in the Oshkosh School system for 35 years on the custodial staff and lives on the west side near the Municipal Golf Course.

Oshkosh's Very Own...
Billy Hoeft

Oshkosh's Billy Hoeft grew up in the same era as Dutch Rennert and Herb Tesch and was a left handed pitcher who played in Major League Baseball for 15 seasons. Pitching for Oshkosh High School and then The Oshkosh Giants, Billy quickly caught the eye of the big league scouts.

Signed in 1950 as an amateur free agent by the Detroit Tigers, Billy pitched his first big league game on April 18, 1952 against the Cleveland Indians. In the two innings he pitched, the rookie southpaw faced seven batters, giving up one hit and walking one in his debut. The Tigers lost that game 5-0 with hall of famer Bob Feller notching the win for the Tribe.

In 1953, his second year in the majors, Billy made the record books by becoming only the fourth American League pitcher and the ninth in major league history to strike out the side with only nine pitches. Facing the Chicago White Sox, Billy fanned Jim Rivera, Mike Fornieles and Chico Carrasquel, a feat that had none been done since 1928 with Left Grove.

In 1955, Billy hit another milestone in his career when he gave up the first career home run to Harmon Killebrew, who would go on to hit 572 more in his journey to the hall of fame. This was a standout season for Hoeft as he was named to the American League All Star team and ranked 16th in voting for AL MVP that year.

Billy Hoeft
Photo Credit: Baseball Reference.com

Hoeft hurled for the Tigers from 1952 to 1959, with 1956 being his best season when he won 20 games as a starter. A remarkable statistic to consider was that of those 20 wins, 18 games were complete games. A complete game is when the starting pitcher pitches the entire game without any help from the bullpen...a feat almost unheard of today.

Billy was traded to the Boston Red Sox in 1959 for only a short time and quickly that same season then dealt to the Baltimore Orioles. Used mainly as a relief pitcher, it was Billy's best year ever closing the 1961 season with a 2.02 ERA.

His professional career started to wind down in 1963 when Baltimore traded Hoeft to San Francisco. Over the next four seasons, Billy made the circuit playing for the Milwaukee Braves (1964), back to the Tigers as a free agent (1965), the Chicago Cubs (1965-66), then back to San Francisco one more time (1966) where he played his final four games as a major leaguer.

Lifetime career stats:

G	W	L	ERA	IP	H	BB	SO	HR	SV
505	97	101	394	1847.1	1820	685	1140	173	33

William Frederick Hoeft was born in Oshkosh on May 17, 1932.

Billy passed away on March 16, 2010 where he lived in Canadian Lakes, Michigan at age 77.

"Donny and Grabo"..the Oshkosh Connection

As mentioned earlier, I joined the Wisconsin National Guard in 1969, just as I was graduating from Oshkosh High. I was 18 years old and not sure what my next moves were. I had really wanted to pursue a career in architectural drafting, but first I needed to complete my 6 month basic training at Ft Leonard Wood, MO. My unit was the 1157 Transportation Company located in Oshkosh. But what in the world does all this have to do with sports, you say? Well, I soon learned after enlisting that members of my unit included two of the newest stars of the Green Bay Packers.

They were known as the "Bonus Babies" of Green Bay Packer Head Coach Vince Lombardi. Donny Anderson and Jim Grabowski were two prime picks from the 1966 NFL draft. Donny was a first round pick out of Texas Tech and "Grabo" a first rounder out of Illinois. Rumor has it Lombardi placed a phone call to then Wisconsin Governor Warren Knowles to get "Grabo" and "The Golden Boy" enlisted in the Guard to avoid losing them to the draft. Some even say Vince went as high as calling President Kennedy. I'm not sure if that is true or not, but those of us from the Lombardi era would not doubt ol' Vince could pull this one off.

So with the recent World Championships (before the name Superbowl was coined), and the Packer legacy growing stronger, these two men were quite a presence. It seemed to some of us more "common folk" that "Andy" and "Grabo" were afforded considerations that we weren't privileged to have. They were really two different characters as persona goes. Jim was more conservative and tried to keep as low profile as possible, just tried to blend in. Donny would "fall in" to formation wearing his aviator style sunglasses and sipping coffee in a white styrofoam cup. His "at ease" posture was also slightly different than what you would consider "regulation", but he had such an aura about him that everyone just thought he was cool.

I don't want to give the wrong impression here. For the record, Donny was always very friendly and approachable. I recall an incident at summer camp one year when I was designated to go to the post ice house and pick up some ice to use to cool our field rations. I went to the ice point and was turned away by a couple of higher ranking NCO's saying our unit already had used our assigned ice rations for the week. I drove back to our company Orderly Room and reported to the First Sergeant I could not get ice. Sitting nearby at a desk, shades on and coffee in hand, sat number 44. Donny overheard my conversation with the "First Shirt" and said "Domer, take me over there". So we hopped in our vehicle and I drove over to the ice point, driving ever so carefully as to not spill any of Donny's coffee.

When we got there, I pulled up next to the building, pulled up the parking brake and shut off the engine. Donny looked over at me and said "Wait here." He climbed out of the truck and sauntered up the concrete steps leading to the office door. He was in there for about 2 minutes when the door swung open and Donny motioned for me to back the truck up to the loading dock. I did as he said and the two guys who refused me earlier started dragging out 50 lb blocks of ice, one after another and loaded them into the cargo bed. As we drove away I asked Donny how he managed to change their mind. He just smiled and said he signed a few autographs. We had enough ice for several days.

Oshkosh's Very Own...

Robert Lautenschlager

This morning I am sitting here enjoying my first cup of coffee, looking out the window over Lake Winnebago and all the non-resident ducks swimming in front of the house. This time of the year we always spot species of ducks we do not normally see here throughout the year. These "transients" are just stopping by on their pilgrimage north to enjoy the summer and raise a new family. This morning they seem to be acting a bid odd as they search for their mate for this season. Karen likes to say they're "*Twitterpated*" this time of year. That's a phrase she's always liked from the Disney movie *Bambi*.

Most of the ducks paddling around out front this morning are Canvasbacks. They're fairly large as ducks go, and brandish white and black bodies with a rusty brownish red head. Canvasbacks move in and out of Lake Winnebago each spring and fall during their migratory journey. With the ice recently gone, the ducks are taking full advantage of open water as they select their mate and continue their journey north.

I notice my coffee cup needs filling and make my way back to the kitchen for a refill. On my way, I glance at an oil painting over our fireplace. The illustrator has captured a flock of Canvasbacks, wings set as they prepare to land on a marshy, ice-covered lake which resembles the landscapes of nearby waters that border Oshkosh. I smile as I think of how often those of us in this area, myself included, take what we have around us for granted. All the things being surrounded by water brings.

The artist of the painting is a local favorite.

Robert Lautenschlager had a special talent and was a wonderful artist in his own right. Local legends say that at one point, Lautenschlager was offered a job by Disney to work as an artist or illustrator.

Robert Lautenschlager

To those who knew him, they called him "Chobby". My efforts to try to find out where the nickname came from were fruitless. I talked to surviving family members Peg Lautenschlager, Jim Backus and Bill Fauk, but to no avail. Surely, there must be someone out there who knows. But that's what I found out. The further I dug, the less I came up with. It seems Lautenschlager was a somewhat private individual.

Robert H. Lautenschlager was born on August 14, 1920...the tenth child of twelve born to John Adam and Elizabeth Lautenschlager.

A single man his entire life, Lautenschlager grew up on Oshkosh's westside and attended Roosevelt School. Lautenschlager descendant and Oshkosh resident Jim Backus shared some interesting family insights with me. "Little information is available on him" Jim related. "There are some newspaper articles I found from the 1930's that report Lautenschlager winning art awards in school with safety poster contests and the sort." Evidence his talent was present at even a very young age.

Former Wisconsin State Attorney General Peg Lautenschlager is Robert's niece and generously shared some information with me from her family memories. Peg's father Milton (Fritz) was Robert's brother. "Robert loved the Roxy and ate there frequently." Peg remembers, as a boy, Robert lived on Sawyer Street, just down from Roosevelt School which he attended as a youth. "He didn't finish high school. He was drafted into the army and served his duty in North Africa. While in the service, he drew cartoons that were widely published." After the war, he returned home and with the help of the GI Bill, enrolled in the Layton School of Art. His attendance there was short lived however, as he told people he wasn't learning anything he didn't already know.

Peg recalled he was always single and loved to dance. He would use his paintings to barter for what he needed or as a gift on special occasions. "Many times, the paintings were still wet when he gave them to the recipient. When he needed some money for dinner, drinks or entertainment, he would just sit down and paint something...usually a wildlife scene as he was able to produce them more quickly with less need for nuance and blending of color." She remembers her uncle as having "a certain naiveté" about him. "His thoughts were not always realistic, but he was a decent soul. I don't think he ever had a negative thought about anyone."

It isn't galleries, shoppes, boutiques or museums where you would find his work. I've been told by many fellow west-siders through the years that when he needed some money, Lautenschlager would sit down, paint a portrait or two, and sell them word of mouth through friends, acquaintances and some of the numerous taverns up and down Main Street.

His works became very popular in the 1960's and 70's with Oshkosh residents. In fact, many of his portraits were featured in one of Oshkosh's most popular supper clubs...Butch's Anchor Inn. Sea captains, shipwrecks, and ships at sea were just a few of the paintings that hung on the wall of this famous eatery.

One of his more impressive works can still be seen today. In 1960's, Lautenschlager was contracted to paint a wall length mural at Shoreview Lanes on Murdock.

Lautenschlager Mural at Shoreview Lanes
Photo Credit: Randy Domer

My research to find what paintings of his might still be in existence took me in several different directions. Mike Miller, manager at Shore View Lanes is proud of the mural that has adorned the wall there for a half century. "I love that painting" Mike shared. "As long as I can

Lautenschlager's Canvasbacks
Photo Credit: Randy Domer

remember, we would contact the museum and they would send someone out to restore the mural every few years." The Shoreview mural has recently started to show signs of needed attention. For his canvas, Lautenschlager used a concrete block wall. Years of moisture and chemicals continue to take their toll.

Next I was pointed in the direction of downtown Main Street. Two doors south of The Magnet Bar is The Distillery Pub. I walked in and found co-owner James Lee tending bar. I introduced myself, pulled up a stool and there it was, as big as day. A beautiful scenic mural of an American Indian, bow and arrow in hand, stepping out of his canoe to hunt his game. James was glad I stopped in. "You know, nobody pays much attention to that thing. I'm glad somebody is interested." Lee said they recently had it cleaned as years of cigarette smoke and dust had darkened the painting. "We had it professionally done...and just a very little touch up painting too." I asked Lee if they had ever considered selling the mural.

"Couldn't do it" James quipped. "Not only because we like it and it's been part of this bar for so long; it's painted directly on the wood paneling on the wall!"

I thanked Lee for his time, information and photos he let me shoot, and then headed out the door to my next stop.

I agreed to meet my friend Jim Senderhauf for lunch that day. Jim suggested we meet at Jansen's on Bowen Street for a sandwich. He also wanted to introduce me to Julie Johnson. Julie works at Jansen's part time as a server and has been working there for years. An author in her own right, Julie wrote a book titled "Oshkosh Down Under," a work on the tunnels that ran underground from the Athearn Hotel and Grand Opera House.

I walked in the door at the appointed time and found Jim already seated at a table in the back of the restaurant. Jim and Julie were already

Lautenschlager's Indian, Distillery Pub, Main St.
Photo Credit: James Lee, April Chase

engaged in deep conversation on the Athearn Hotel. Jim introduced me to Julie as I casually mentioned something about my morning's journey and quest to find Lautenschlager's surviving pieces.

"Well then you'll be glad you stopped here" Julie commented. She pointed over my shoulder to the wall opposite the bar. "We have one right here!" she exclaimed. I had been in this restaurant numerous times and remember seeing the mural, but had not connected it to Lautenschlager.

Owner Brad Cobb was there, so I asked him about the painting. "It was here when I bought the place" Brad remarked. Upon closer examination, I saw a date (1961) painted in the lower corner. According to Peg Lautenschlager, it was common for Lautenschlager to date his murals, but not individual paintings or portraits. The mural depicts a number of European looking men and women making merriment around a long table with food and drink.

Other large murals like this were done by Lautenschlager through the years and have been lost to time. I'm told the old Reeve Memorial

Lautenschlager, Painted 1961, Jansen's, Bowen St
Photo Courtesy: Brad Cobb

Union on the campus of UWO had a mural, but it was lost when the building was razed.

There may be more out there…there probably are. People I know that own "a Lautenschlager" say so with the same enthusiasm as if it were a Renoir or Monet. They are always proud of what they have.

On January 2, 1975, Robert Lautenschlager died of a heart attack on Main Street. He was 54 years old.

"Chobby" Lautenschlager was truly one of the people that make Oshkosh what it is today.

The Children's Day Parade

One of my favorite memories of growing up and living in Oshkosh was the annual Children's Day Parade.

Sponsored and organized by the Ohio Street Civic Association, the parade is a city favorite that features kids and home built floats, bikes and wagons. Each is decorated with crepe paper, homemade signs and usually constructed by the kids themselves, along with a little help from mom or dad in some cases.

The parade originally assembled at Sacred Heart School and traveled on 5th Street to Ohio Street and then to South Park. Later the parade assembled at Old Franklin School Park and went down 6th street to Ohio Street and then to South Park Street and into South Park. At the completion of the parade, each participant is given a bag of treats, followed by a picnic with games, food, music and prizes.

The Ohio Street Civic Association was organized in 1933 by small businessmen in the sixth Ward to promote civic minded activity, and good fellowship for the betterment of the community. Originally, membership was limited to Ohio Street Merchants, but soon after expanded to include other Oshkosh businesses throughout the city. My uncle Neil Ziebell was one of those merchants. Co-owner of Schneider and Ziebell's Standard on 8th and Ohio, Neil and Herb supported the Association and promoted the parade. My parents would take us there, park their car in Neil's station, and we would sit on the curb across from Nigl's Bakery and Punky's Bar to watch the parade.

The Association was pivotal in financially supporting various projects including the Wisconsin Ave Bridge, paving of Ohio Street, ornamental lighting on Ohio Street, bleachers at local ball diamonds, digging the South Park well, constructing the kiddies' wading pool, flagpole, benches, playground equipment and shade trees in South Park.

The Children's Day Parade

The Children's Day Parade rolls past the Hi Holder on 5th and Knapp St
Photo credit: Dan Radig

The Association also sponsored and dedicated the monument in South Park to Oshkosh soldiers who lost their lives in WWII.

In the 1950's and 60's, my wife, Karen, recalls building parade floats with her cousins. Her uncle, Tony Sosnoski, was always willing and able to assist the kids by providing wagons and the means to transport the float along the parade route. In 1960, they chose to adopt the theme of introducing the two new states to join the Union - Alaska and Hawaii. The float's theme was "Meet the two new stars" Karen was Miss Alaska and a friend was Miss Hawaii. With the help of Uncle Tony, the kids took a wagon, some plywood, crepe paper, Kleenex and toilet paper to decorate the float. Karen remembers finishing in the top three that year.

Another year they dressed up her cousin Dianne Sosnoski as the Statue of Liberty, while Karen, dressed as a sailor, pulled the float.

Each year, one or two local merchants would ride in a truck throwing candy to the families lined up and down the street. Kids would scramble and make a mad dash to get what they could.

At the end of the parade, everyone made their way into South Park where games, food and refreshments were served. Many families came early to "stake out" their very own picnic areas. Karen's clan, the Sosnoskis, always made this a big occasion with the entire family. They would usually arrive early in the morning and stake out the area by the horseshoe pits. Nobody enjoyed a good game of horseshoes more than that bunch! The men would pair up, horseshoe in one hand and a glass of beer in the other. The horseshoes would fly hitting the sand followed by hoots and hollers as the heat of competition rose.

Each family brought portable grills and charcoal. They even brought dishes to share with each woman having her own specialty…potato salad, baked beans, peanut squares…brats, burgers and hot dogs for the little ones were standard fare. And of course, Uncle Harold "Pee Wee" Brown, who worked for a local beer distributor, would arrange to tap a "pony barrel" of beer for the occasion.

On this very special day, South Park was a bee hive of activity as families spent the entire day picnicking and watching the children play on the swings and in the kiddies pool. Smoke from the dozens of charcoal grills filled the air. Music was provided by local bands like the VFW Band or one of the nearby schools.

A splendid time was had by all.

Downtown

In the 1950's, the downtown area was the heartbeat of the city. Main Street was the business district for all major retailers and small businesses alike. Shopping malls had not yet emerged and the city of Oshkosh was beginning to sprawl.

Everything you wanted was on or near Main Street. Some of my favorite childhood memories happened the first Friday of the month. The first of the month is when many of our household bills were due. The mortgage, telephone and utility bills along with the occasional "layaway" payment that was due. Layaways were common then. Retailers like JC Penneys, Klines, Johnson Hills, etc. would accept a small down payment to hold an item you wanted to buy, but didn't have the means to pay for it in full. Credit cards were not yet introduced into the mainstream so layaway allowed you to make payments on the item each week until it was fully paid. Then you could take it home. Today, we pay our bills by credit card, a check in the mail or with electronic bill paying over the internet. As a youth, I remember when my dad came home from work on that first Friday, we would all pile into the car and drive downtown. Our first stop was the Oshkosh Savings and Loan on Washington to pay the mortgage. At night, the sidewalks alongside the Savings and Loan would sparkle like diamonds. Then it was over to Mueller Potter or Public Service, whichever was most convenient, to pay the gas and light bill. The First National Bank was where my parents did some of their banking then, along with the Savings and Loan, of course. We each had our own "Christmas Club" where 25 cents a week added up to some big money come the end of October. We'd wait for that Christmas Club check to come in the mail, and then we could start shopping. As kids, that was enough money to buy a small gift for my parents, brother and sister.

Downtown was bustling with shoppers and so busy we often had a difficult time finding a parking space. If we could find a spot without a meter, or at least one with a meter with some time left on it, we were lucky!

The big retailers were the department stores. Kline's, Johnson Hills, Newman's, Sears Roebuck and JC Penney's were the retail giants. "Dime Stores" were the place to go for just about anything from bobby pins to greeting cards. The name was derived from the late 19th century when stores like this sold just about everything for 5 or 10 cents. Oshkosh had four such stores…WT Grant, JJ Newberry, S.S. Kresge and F.W. Woolworth's. Several of these "dime stores" had lunch counters. I loved to sit at the counter on a revolving stool, and take respite from shopping with a meatloaf sandwich, fountain soda or ice cream sundae. One could even purchase a pet as choices of parakeets, goldfish and baby turtles were available along with all the supplies to sustain them.

The Continental was the premier men's clothing store on Main St. You could buy a suit, rent a tux for a wedding, or if you needed a Boy Scout or Cub Scout uniform, The Continental had it.

The Exclusive Company was one of my favorite stores as it provided all of my music needs under one roof. I spent most of my hard earned dollars as a teen there buying 45 RPM records, albums and stereo equipment. My buddy, Garrett Galica and I stopped by there at least once a week. Before we could drive, we would walk to the bus stop on the corner of Sawyer St and Adams Avenue, and take the bus downtown. It dropped us off only a block away from The Exclusive Company. I would estimate I bought (and still own) a couple hundred 45's and albums during those years. Albums were made of vinyl and played at 33 1/3 rpm. They were sold in both stereo and Monoraul format with stereo costing one dollar more. Most albums sold for $4.99 and 45 rpm records were .99 each. Mr. (James A.) Giombetti was the President and Mr. Al Martin ran the store on Main, just north of the First National Bank and next to Osco Drug. "Mr. G" was famous for his radio commercials where he would aggressively promote their products…Albums, CD's and stereo equipment. He would always end his ad with the phrase *"…say it with me…The Exclusive Company…downtown Oshkosh!"* Both men always greeted me by name and made me feel special. I imagine I was probably one of their best customers for a few years.

Located near The Exclusive Company was the Caramel Crisp Shop. A downtown fixture since 1933, Caramel Crisp's mouth watering caramel corn was to die for. As you walked past the store, the aroma of fresh popped popcorn combined with the sweet smell of hot caramel filled the air. Once you started eating caramel corn, you could not stop. Through the years, they did business in several different locations, including next to the Oshkosh Theater and today near the old Park Plaza mall site.

Many key businesses thrived just a block or two off Main. Oshkosh B'Gosh, Guernsey Dairy Company, The Oshkosh Daily Northwestern, The Athearn Hotel…just to name a few.

As you drove north on Main Street, you passed through the business district where Gibson Chevrolet occupied nearly an entire block, while Badger Oldsmobile stood proudly on the "Rocket Corner" (Main and Irving). These were two of the largest car dealerships in Oshkosh. Several pizza parlors like Louarti's, Jess and Nick's, the Red Lantern not only had delicious pizza, but provided a gathering place for teens. The Sunlite Dairy in the 700 block of N. Main Street had delicious ice cream cones. Unlike area drive ins, Sunlite was an Ice Cream Parlor. You walked into the store and along the wall was a long freezer case filled with assorted flavors of ice cream. A few small tables invited guests to sit, relax and enjoy their cone. My favorite flavor was black cherry.

Angers Jewelers did business at 69 Main Street and could easily be found by the giant clock that stood right out front. The Oshkosh National Bank Building on the corner of Main and Waugoo Streets, kept eveyone up to date on changing weather conditions by means of a large beacon placed on the roof with colored lights that indicated current or changing conditions. A red light means warmer, green colder, yellow no change and when the ball at the beacon's top flashed it meant rain or snow was about to fall (1) . This was advanced technology for the 1950's.

Several ladies shops were located up and down Main. Jeffrey's was very popular with teens, while Mangels, Christiansen's and Dickson's catered to more mature women and businesswomen. My friend's mother, Jean Zimmerman, owned and operated Dickson's with her brother and business partner, Dick Fink.

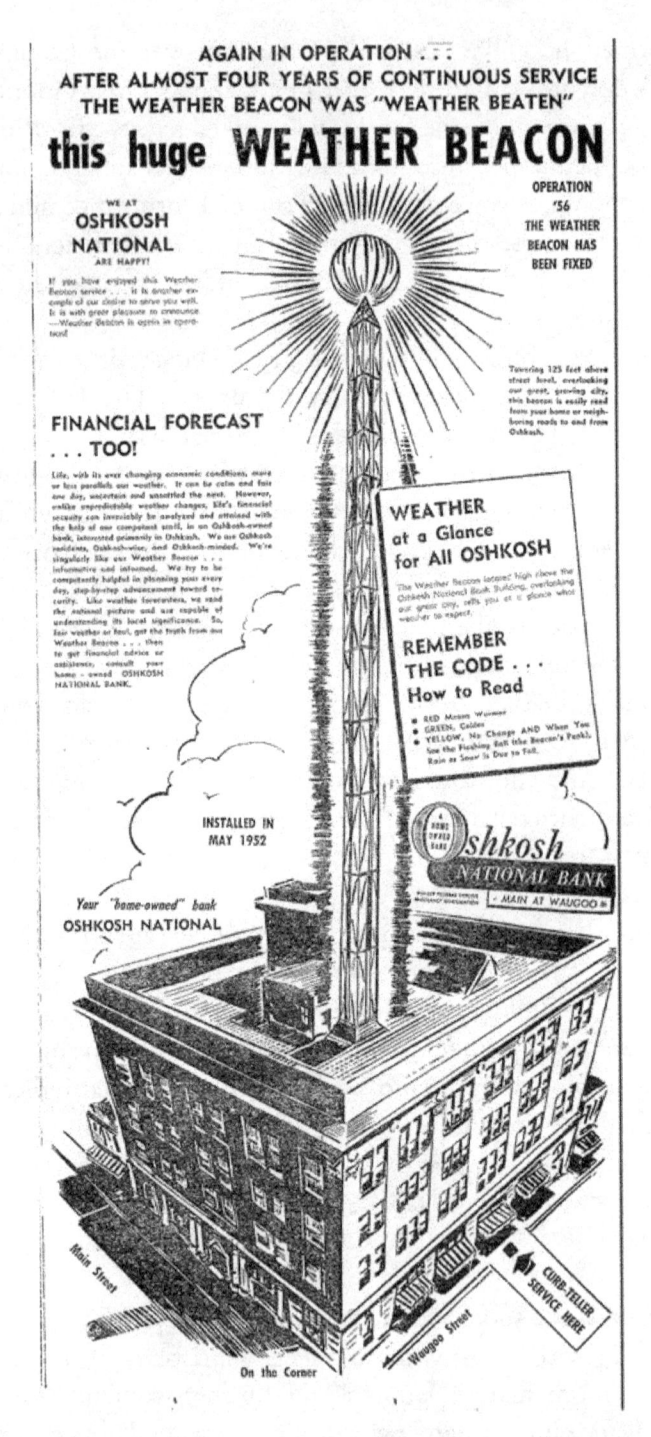

(1) (Source: Oshkosh Daily Northwestern, April 9, 1956, page 3)

Dickson's began doing business on August 17, 1939. Jean's parents, Herb and Irma Fink decided to open a women's shop as Irma was an expert seamstress and Jean, now a young lady, had expressed her interest in art and colors. Herb was an experienced businessman, previously owning a radio sales and service company called *Fink Company* on South Main Street, two doors north of Ninth Avenue in the mid 1930's.

Dickson's original location opened at 7 Merritt Street, one half block east of Main. It was a one room store, but suited the needs of the business at the time. Herb decided he wanted to expand the business in 1944, so they increased their occupancy toward Main Street and moved the main entrance to the corner of Main and Merritt. Jean recalls "My dad did all the expansion and remodeling work himself. The fixtures, the flooring…everything!".

Jean would work in the store when her husband Roy was home to watch their two kids. The store featured the latest in ladies fashions including handbags, hats, hosiery, slips, nightwear, dresses coats and sportswear.

Then, in 1965, Herb and Irma decided to retire. Jean and her brother Dick took over the business and ran it until Valentine's Day of 1970. (coincidentally Valentine's Day is also Jean's birthday) Park Plaza was being built at the time, and it was becoming clear that the downtown area was starting to erode. They faced the difficult decision whether or not to compete. Rather than choose to re-locate or expand, Jean and Dick decided to close the business.

The fate of Dickson's was not unlike many other small businesses on Main Street that saw the new Park Plaza indoor mall moving foot traffic away from their business. If you fast forward from here, eventually the same fate befell Park Plaza when commercial businesses moved west to the frontage road areas along US Highway 41.

Today, Oshkosh is still working hard to rebuild businesses in downtown. It is a daunting task, but slowly we are seeing a glimmer of light of restoring today what once was a thriving shopping destination. Small boutiques add that small town charm. The Farmers Market in the summer months is very popular with people who want fresh fruits and vegetables with the feel of an open air marketplace. Recently, Hollywood visited downtown Oshkosh and filmed "Public Enemy" starring Johnny Depp and Christian Bale, much to the interest and delight of locals.

Activities like Galley Walk, the Leach Amphitheater and free outdoor movie night are also attracting people back into the downtown area. The restoration of the historic Grand Opera House in Monument Square and The Morgan House off Main St. on Church Avenue help us keep that nostalgic feeling as we embrace the past.

Oshkosh is facing some interesting challenges along the river however. The Convention Center and adjoining hotel are vacant, but a recent agreement with local investors and the University of Wisconsin intend to breathe life back into their existence. Buildings along the river have been torn down and the land left barren at this time. The green space that was created is inviting locals to the waterfront to walk along its banks and enjoy the view, listen to music or even drop in a line and fish.

The Pioneer Inn was a beautiful stately business at the mouth of the Fox River. Built in 1965, it was one of Oshkosh's premier businesses in its day. The property featured a 150 room hotel, 3 restaurants, a 250 boat marina complete with sea plane area and facilities to host weddings, receptions and meetings. Passenger boats, the Ki Ni Island Queen and Pioneer Princess, offered excursions onto Lake Winnebago and along the Fox River.

But plans to raze the property and build permanent, more modern living accommodations were thwarted by political red tape and the DNR. Ki-Ni Island is now a deserted pile of rubble (remnants of fill from the demolition of another historic landmark, The Athearn Hotel in 1964). A deserted shell of the lobby and restaurant area and the marina are the only remaining evidence of this once glorious landmark.

Those of us that cherish those nostalgic memories of the old downtown, embrace it's revitalization, and anxiously await for its re emergence to take us back to a time when things were …well let's just say more simple.

Television and Radio

Imagine watching TV today with no color picture. Or having to get up and manually turn the channel or adjust the volume. How about only having three channels to watch?

That's what television was like in the 1950's.

My earliest memory of television was about 1955. My parents had a black and white TV in a small modest console with four spindle type legs and doors that closed when you weren't watching it. On our roof was a TV antenna that was connected to a rotor that sat perched on top of the TV set. The rotor would operate the antenna and turn it directionally to get the best picture possible. The antenna was installed by Bud Lowell, who eventually became Sherriff of Winnebago County. Antennas with a rotor were a step up from "rabbit ears". Rabbit ears were two telescoping antenna's that were joined together at the base and connected to the television by wire, thus forming a "rabbit ears" appearance. You would turn the rabbit ears in various directions until you found the best reception. If the picture was still not clear, you would add small sheets of aluminum foil to the tip of each antenna.

There were only three television stations within reach of Oshkosh, each located in Green Bay. The national network affiliates then were CBS (channel 2 -WBAY), NBC (channel 5- WFRV) and ABC (channel 11-WLUK). Channel selection eventually grew with the onset of PBS and other locally broadcast channels. Programming on PBS then was very limited. The only programs they broadcasted worth watching were geared toward small children. *Romper Room* and *Sesame Street* were the most popular children's programs. They were both entertaining and educational.

On a clear day, you could play around with the rotor and get some Milwaukee channels. Channel 4, WTMJ in Milwaukee broadcast the

Sunday Funnies on Sunday morning. A narrator would read the comic strips out of the Sunday Milwaukee Journal while the camera panned across the comic strip.

Sometimes, Green Bay Packer games could only be seen on the Milwaukee channels as they were blacked out in Green Bay on home games in Green Bay. If the home game was played at County Stadium in Milwaukee, it would be broadcast on the Green Bay stations.

Reception of Milwaukee channels was always suspect at best. I would watch my dad try to fine tune the rotor so we could watch the Milwaukee telecast of the Packer games. The picture would go from totally obscure and fuzzy to making out silhouettes if you squinted just right. He would fiddle around until he got it best he could, then we would sit back and try to watch as the picture faded in and out. Each time it went out, my dad would curse, and start pushing the white tab on top of the rotor again. This would go on until either we were able to watch the game, or just gave up in frustration.

TV stations did not broadcast 24 hours a day like most do today. At the end of their programming day (and at the beginning), a picture of an American Flag would be displayed as The Star Spangled Banner played, signaling the end, or sometimes the beginning of the broadcast day. At the end of the National Anthem, a test pattern would come onto the screen with a long, constant beeping sound.

With all programming being broadcast and televised in black and white, some companies invented little gimmicks to try to simulate color. Plastic sheets were designed to "fool the eye" with rainbow colors of blue on the top (because skies were blue) and green on the bottom (because grass was green) even if the program you were watching had no sky or grass. The plastic sheet clung to the screen of the TV and would peel right off if you didn't want it on.

In the late 1950's I saw my first color television. My Uncle, Neil Ziebell, bought one and it was a beauty! We were invited over to watch it and I remember it vividly. *Bonanza* was one of first programs to telecast "...in living color on NBC". The NBC peacock was born and TV viewing was changed forever. The Cartwrights never looked so good! "The Wonderful World of Disney" was another of our early color favorites as Walt Disney hosted wonderful family programming and classic Disney cartoons.

Russ Weidow as Colonel Caboose
Photo Credit: Jim Backus, FB

After school at 3:30pm, we would rush home to watch Colonel Caboose and The Popeye Cartoon Theater. On Saturday morning it was Tom and Jerry, Beany and Cecil, Tom Terrific, King Leonardo and a host of various cartoon characters. My dad's favorite programs were The Honeymooners with Jackie Gleason and The Untouchables. Since they were his favorites, they were mine too! Baseball games were only on Saturday afternoons. Joe Garagiola, Pee Wee Reese and Dizzy Dean reported all the action.

For the first few decades of television, there were no remote controls. All station and functioning changes were made manually. If the channel knob, which was made of high grade plastic, broke or was stripped, a needle nose pliers was a useful tool to have to change channels.

No DVR's, VCR's, DVD players or internet downloads existed in those days. People watched what was on, when it was on, or you didn't see it. If a movie was desired, you went to the theater downtown.

Commercials didn't ban cigarette ads back then. *The Marlboro Man* was iconic. You'd *walk a mile for a Camel*, and *Winston taste good, like a cigarette should*. The Hamm's Bear entertained us *from the land of sky blue waters...* while Schlitz was *the beer that made Milwaukee famous*.

The programming guide was not a menu that scrolled across your screen. It was either purchase a TV Guide weekly or tear the TV listings from the Oshkosh Daily Northwestern.

Our local radio station in the 50's was WOSH, 1490 on the dial. FM radio had not yet come on the scene, so AM was the standard, and only, radio broadcast media. One benefit with AM radio is that it has a farther reaching broadcast area than FM and we loved listening to the Milwaukee (WOKY) and Chicago (WBBM) stations. In the evening, around 6pm, the FCC made some stations lower their broadcast frequency. That meant large city markets like Chicago, St Louis, Minneapolis and sometimes even Cleveland could be heard due to their stronger signals.

WOSH had a promotion called "Red Rover" where a local DJ and station personality Tom Miles, and other WOSH DJ's would drive around the city and stop randomly in front of a house. The station, between songs, would call out to Red Rover and ask where they were. The roving DJ would say something like, "I'm in front of 621 North Sawyer and if the occupant comes out in the next two minutes, I have a number of wonderful gifts and prizes!" It was fun to see the red station wagon with the WOSH logo emblazoned on the sides drive around and hoping just maybe, they were headed to our house.

Local resident and Oshkosh historian Dan Radig shared this memory with me. "I won the Red Rover prize package when I was 10. They drove up to the house and handed me a pile of gift certificates and 8-packs of Pepsi, Peoples Beer and Chief Oshkosh… the 'mother lode' for a 10 year old!"

The television experience has changed drastically since then. We now have a 65- inch plasma, 3D TV with a sound system that carries into every room. It all comes into the house on a 3/8 inch cable, direct from a satellite. We now can receive almost 200 channels with a couple of dozen dedicated to nothing but music. If you want, you can subscribe and get every single NFL, NBA, NHL or Major League Baseball game played at any time. And here's the best part…it all works by remote! My music now comes from a satellite or downloaded from I-Tunes to play on my computer or IPOD. The music is digital (remember when stereo was a big deal?) and the sound quality superb.

I have loads of fun memories of radio and television from "the good old days", but please, don't ask me to give up any of my new audio visual toys!

Oshkosh's Very Own...

RALPH A. OTT

Born April 11, 1923 as the second oldest of seven children, Ralph Ott grew up on the south side of Oshkosh in the area of Fifth Street between Sawyer and Knapp Streets. Ralph was the son of Clarence and Agnes Ott and my mother's older and only brother...and my uncle. Sister Loretta was the eldest, then Ralph, Phyllis, Geraldine (my mother), Joyce, Jackie and Sandra made up the Ott clan.

Growing up as southsiders, these kids made the area around Sacred Heart Church and the neighborhoods their play ground. My Aunt Loretta remembers playing with brother Ralph and the neighborhood gang around Fifth Street. "In those days, there was no television or computer games to occupy our time.

We made our own fun playing outside until the street lights came on". Loretta just recently celebrated her 90th birthday and still lives in her home on the west side of town. "I remember one time, Ralph put a frog down a neighbor girl's shirt and she screamed a fit!" She said with a chuckle "I still remember that...Ralph was a *stinker* sometimes".

Ralph liked to hangout with his friends Carl Sosnoski and Harold Frank. His girlfriend and sweetheart was Dorothy Wolf. Ralph attended Franklin School as a youth, but never attended high school. He chose then to work rather than go to school as many kids that age were doing in the 1930's and early 40's, so he never received a high school diploma. In the early 1940's, Ralph took a job with the Paine Lumber Company, located just off Algoma Boulevard on the east side of the river and near the Paine Thrift Bank.

At 17 years old, Ralph decided to join the CCC (Civilian Conservation Corps). He enrolled on July 17, 1940 at Camp Crystal Lake in Minocqua Wisconsin to begin his service to the Corps. As a teenager, Ralph's physical description, according to his discharge papers,

Loretta, Ralph (kneeling), Geraldine, Jackie, Phyllis, Joyce, Sandra (sitting), Clarence
Photo Credit: Randy Domer

Ralph A. Ott

was: blue eyes, blonde hair, light complexion and five feet-six inches tall. He was honorably discharged from the CCC on December 23, 1940. At about this same time, the war was escalating in Europe. The Germans continued to increase their occupation of most of Eastern Europe and France and were continuing to advance with Great Britain in their gun sights. Ralph joined the Army on March 2, 1943. His family, friends and girlfriend Dorothy were at the train station that day to see him off.

PFC Ralph A. Ott was assigned to the 112 Infantry, 28th division US Army.

While serving his country, Ralph's letters home talked of missing the days fishing with his dad. He wrote "Dad always pulled them up left and right, I sat there without hardly a bite...he would laugh and tease me about it." He longed for the day he would return home to Oshkosh where his brother-in-law Neil Ziebell had a cottage on the Fox River and a new boat that prompted Ralph to ask Neil "...send me some pictures of the boat and cottage so I can look at them once in awhile and remember what's waiting for me back home." In his letters to his sisters, he would always ask about each one, worrying the most about the littlest ones, as their mother had passed away just the year previous.

The infamous "D-Day Invasion" occurred on the Sixth of June, 1944. Ralph's unit, The 28th Infantry Division was stationed in Great Britain on that historical day. Ralph's unit left England on July 24th and established its headquarters on Omaha Beach. *(1) "In the aftermath of the Operation COBRA breakout, American forces were advancing rapidly into France. The 28th Infantry Division moved out to catch up with and support this advance. On July 30, it assisted Combat Command A of the 2nd Armored Division and 29th Infantry Division in their successful defense of Villebaudon against German counter attacks. The following day, July 31, they assumed responsibility for its own sector of the front just north of Percy.*

The 28th Infantry Division attacked to seize Percy, and secured the town on August 1. From this point, it continued its attack southeast, advancing through difficult terrain and stubborn resistance. By August 4, the division had pushed another 8 miles further into Saint-Sever-Calvados. This put the 28th Infantry Division and the 9th Infantry Division on its right flank, in effective control of the Foret de St. Sever. American possession of this forest denied the German defenders excellent cover and concealment, and numerous points of observation they had come to depend upon. It also positioned the Americans to control an extensive road network"

(1) (Source: American Battle Monuments Commission, 2008)

It was here on French soil, midway between Avranches and Flers, on August 5, 1944, PFC Ralph A. Ott was mortally wounded by German gunfire and died. At 21 years of age, Ralph had given the ultimate sacrifice for his country…his life.

The day is Wednesday, August 23, 1944. Back home in Oshkosh, it was a normal day. Looking around town, one would hardly know that half a world away, a war was going on. The traffic was moving up and down Main Street, city buses were following their regular routes. The temperature on this day would reach a high of 77 degrees, very comfortable for this time year. Busy shoppers walked from store to store and workers were on their way to their jobs, just like every other day. Car radios were playing the number one hit by Bing Crosby "Swinging on a Star" while billboards at the Strand Theater promoted Cecil B. DeMille's latest feature "The Story of Dr. Wassell" starring Gary Cooper.

Harold Juedes was at his desk at the telegram office on Algoma Blvd when his instrument began printing out a telegram. Juedes read the telegram and noticed it was addressed to Clarence Ott. As telegrams go, there is no privacy or confidentiality, so Harold immediately was aware of the news of Ralph's death. He knew the Ott family well, so Harold quickly jumped into his car and drove to the Tankar Station on Jackson Ave. where he knew my Uncle Neil Ziebell was working, showed him the telegram, then made his way over to Fifth Street to deliver the tragic news to Ralph's father, Clarence. Neil left work and drove over to the Deltox where his wife Loretta worked and delivered the sad news to her about her brother. Neil and Loretta then drove together over to her dad's house to be with him and the family.

Ralph was buried in a temporary US Military Cemetery, near where he had fallen along with his fellow comrades in arms that had also lost their life in this battle. This cemetery, Le Chêne -Guerin, was located about 14 miles south of St. Lô France.

In 1949, a letter was sent to the family informing them that "the remains of your loved one have been permanently interred" in the Brittany American Cemetery, St. James, France. It is there where Ralph's body rests today along with 4,410 Americans who also lost their lives in this war. Keep in mind, this is just one of several American Cemeteries in Europe holding vigil over our war dead. In the process of re-interment, the family was given the opportunity to bring their loved ones home. I am told that in Ralph's case, the family decided it was best for him to remain where he had been laid to rest in France.

On January 23, 1945, the Purple Heart was posthumously awarded to the Ott family on Ralph's behalf. Today, Ralph's Purple Heart is in my safe keeping, cherished as a reminder to never forget the sacrifice he made. In his honor, every first male child born by his sisters, have been christened with the middle name Ralph. I am proud to be known by this; it is something I have carried and talked about my entire life. When middle names come up, I proudly tell people about my special middle name.

Ralph's Gravesite in Brittany American Cemetery, St. James France

In 2007, I traveled to France with my wife, daughter Brooke and my sister Deb Heidl. During our trip, we made special plans to find the St. James Brittany American Cemetery and locate Ralph's grave. Brooke had been to France a few years prior to this and the French family that was hosting her brought her there at that time. The cemetery is most beautiful, with lush green grassy areas, all perfectly manicured. Tree lined boulevards accent the pure white marble markers of each American hero. The cemetery is overseen and operated by retired American military personnel who take great care, pride and respect in their assigned duties.

Upon our arrival, we were warmly greeted at the entrance gate by a caretaker, a retired US Serviceman, who escorted us into the office to sign in and get information. We explained the reason for our visit, and then were invited to follow our escort out the door. He stopped nearby to pick up a few things, then quickly again we were on our way. We walked along the roadway, careful to not walk across the grass out of respect. We went directly to Plot A, then down to Row 10 and Grave 4. As we approached the grave, the name Ralph A. Ott, etched delicately in the white marble, started to become apparent. The man whose namesake is mine and all the stories I had been told over the years came flooding back.

The beautiful white marble crosses that mark each grave are difficult to read, so our escort knelt down next to the marker and dipped his hand into a small pail. He came up with a handful of wet sand and slowly spread it over the engraving on the cross. He then took a damp sponge and carefully wiped the cross clean, but the sand stayed in the engraving. Ralph's name, rank, etc suddenly became very clear. "We do this, so when you take a photo, the name can be clearly seen", the caretaker quietly explained. He continued, "The sand is from Omaha Beach. We do this to honor all who had fallen on that historic day." The caretaker then stepped back and invited us to come forward. We took photos of family members we brought from home and taped them to the cross…pictures of Ralph, his parents and sisters. We placed a bouquet of fresh flowers we had purchased in a little French flower shop in the nearby town of St. James at the base of the marker.

Next, I presented Ralph with an honor long overdue him. I brought his Purple Heart with us and carefully placed it on the cross alongside his picture. It was the first time Ralph and the Purple Heart had ever been together. As I did this, I was filled with a strong sense of pride and my emotions welled up inside me. I looked back to see it had the same effect on everyone, including our hosting French family.

At this point, we all stepped back from the grave and the caretaker reached into his pocket and pressed a button. Out of the nearby chapel tower came the sound of a bugle playing taps. We were all overcome with emotions and a sense of gratitude for the sacrifice he made; thoughts of how our family felt so many years ago when the news arrived of the loss of their beloved son and brother. I watched cemetery workers stop what they were doing, put down their tools, removing their hat and placing it over their hearts. It was one of the most touching things I have ever experienced.

On the Northeast corner of South Park, on Ohio Street, stands a memorial, erected by The Ohio Street Civic Association to honor Oshkosh heroes that lost their lives in WWII. Next time you are by there, stop for a moment, look for Ralph's name, and maybe say a prayer for Ralph and all those who gave the ultimate sacrifice for our freedom.

Let them know… we will never forget.

Theaters

My earliest recollection on Oshkosh movie theaters starts in the mid 1950's. The Raulf (formerly The Strand), Time, Grand, Mode and Oshkosh Theaters were operating along with the 44 Outdoor Theater. A program through school made it possible to purchase Saturday matinee passes which included series entertainment like "Francis, The Talking Mule". These tickets only cost a dime. Some theaters even offered free admission with Elba Queen canned goods labels! Double features were not uncommon. And that even included a cartoon or two or a Three Stooges short as well! The city bus was our usual form of transportation downtown. The Raulf, Time, Oshkosh and Grand were all located within a few blocks of each other, right on or just off Main Street. We would board the bus on Sawyer, one block south of Roosevelt School and get off near The First National Bank on Main Street. We could then easily walk to any of the four theaters. After the show, we took the bus back home or if it was toward evening, one of our parents would pick us up.

Back then theaters only had one screen. Typically, they would have a Feature (or sometimes a double feature), a sub feature and a couple of cartoons (usually Tom and Jerry or Woody Woodpecker) or movie shorts featuring The Three Stooges, Laurel and Hardy or The Dead End Kids in between. If you arrived in your seat early, you would be treated to coming attractions and ads for local businesses and animated boxes of popcorn and soda pop danced across the screen inviting you go out to the lobby for refreshments. The countdown sequence would start at about ten minutes before the show was to begin. "The show will start in five minutes…" a booming voice would announce. Newsreels were a little before my time, but if you are a few years older than me, you will remember them well. When the cartoons would come on, the audience, mostly kids, would clap and cheer! It was always a very interactive experience between the film and movie goers. When Roy Rogers would catch the bad guys, the audience would erupt in applause and cheers.

The Raulf

Renowned as "The Tallest Building in Oshkosh", the Raulf Hotel is located on the east side of Main Street, just north of Church Avenue. In its day, The Raulf Hotel was a very fine establishment. It was known for having nice accommodations, including an elegant restaurant and even a bowling alley! By the 50's, the hotel's reputation slipped to housing those less fortunate.

The Concession Stand at the Raulf Theater
Photo Credit: Dan Radig

The Raulf was my favorite theater. It seemed to be larger than the other theaters in town. After entering the main door, a long, red carpeted ramp or walkway led to the place where everyone was greeted by a ticket seller. You would purchase your ticket, and then proceed a little further up the long ramp. There, a ticket taker took your ticket, tore it in half and gave you back the stub. Many people may remember Louie Collins who made the Main Street theater circuit pretty regularly. As a boy, I thought Louie was employed by the theaters, but later discovered he was simply a resident visitor who enjoyed hanging out at the local theaters.

The concession stand was not much different than today. Delicious popcorn salted, with or without butter was the big seller. The usual soft drinks were available and the boxes of candy were mostly the same ones you see today. Malted Milk Balls and Good 'N Plenty were among my favorites.

Most theaters would close the balcony areas with a heavy velvet cord unless it was a feature of great popularity. One example that clearly comes to mind took place in the mid 1960's. The Beatles were sweeping America and the new release of *A Hard Day's Night* was showing at The Raulf. The theater was sold out! Once the main seating area was nearly full, they opened the balcony and filled it as well. I remember the girls all screaming during the film, it was unlike anything I'd ever seen. Beatlemania was here. Not since Elvis was there such excitement and frenzy over a rock n roll star. The "English Invasion" was in full swing. No musical group had ever made a full length movie before, and the kids went crazy!

The Time

One block south of The Raulf and two doors from *Jeffrey's* was The Time Theater. The Time was a bit smaller with fewer seats than The Raulf.

Time Theater, Main Street circa 1970's
Photo Credit: Dan Radig/Facebook

Located at 445 N. Main St., the theater came into existence in 1908 according to the city directory and was named *The Superba*. . The entire block was destroyed by fire in 1874 and rebuilding started the same year. In 1911, the name was changed to *The Rex* and Oshkosh had the very first picture show here in 1912. In 1949, the name was changed to the Time Theater. The Time closed as a movie theater in October, 1991.

Currently, the Community Theater Group of Oshkosh, Inc. is the operational and governing board: a non-profit organization with a vision for promoting the arts in Oshkosh and the Fox Valley area. Tax deductable donations to support the theater can be made on their website at www.timecommunitytheater.com

The Grand

On the corner of High Ave and Market Street sits a stately old building. History tells us of a time when performers like Lillian Russell, the Marx Brothers and others graced its stage. It was a glorious thing of beauty, as far as buildings go. Built in 1883, the Grand Opera House attracted celebrities and Presidents alike. William Howard Taft even made an appearance. It was designed by local architect William Waters in a European style with Victorian décor. Beautiful designs and artwork on the ceiling and walls made the Grand Opera House one of the most beautiful venues in the country.

As I was doing my research on the history of this magnificent old theater, I was introduced to a person who not only wrote her own book on the area downtown, but also has a deep seated interest in the history of The Grand as well. Julie Krysiak Johnson, author of *Oshkosh Down Under*, a book that explores the underground tunnels in the areas downtown, agreed to meet with me when she heard of the research I was doing. Julie keeps herself busy working more than one part time job and is the President of the Winnebago County Historical Society.

After conversing with Julie, and recounting all the history Julie has uncovered in her endless efforts to learn more about our city's history, I invited Julie to join me by writing about the early performers who played at the Grand Opera House in its early days. Julie, who and has invested countless hours of research including combing hundreds of old newspapers on The Grand, eagerly accepted.

Julie writes...

The new Grand Opera House in Oshkosh opened its doors to the public on Thursday evening, August 9, 1883 with Robert Marsh as lessee and manager and Jacob Litt as the associate manager. On March 6, 1882, a "stock company composed of as many Oshkosh citizens as wished," (1) had been formed. From there, a new committee was then appointed to raise subscriptions for the erection of the Opera House. The Oshkosh Opera House Association was formed and with its subscribers became owners of the building and enterprise. "The house lacked nothing as regards to comfort, beauty, safety and convenience. Interior decorations and completeness of detail were not excelled in the state."(2) For the opening of the new opera house, special performances were planned by the Opera House Association, with the proceeds to benefit solely the Association fund. These special performances were not to be confused with the general opening of the theater season which took place Saturday, September 1, 1883.

The C. D. Hess Acme Opera Co., presenting English Opera, gave four grand performances starting Thursday evening, August 9, 1883, with three evening performances and a Saturday matinee. "Bohemian Girl" (3) starring Fond du Lac native Abbie Beeson Carrington was the first play performed on the Oshkosh stage. A "literary and musical entertainment" (4) by Guy Lindaley interspersed with various other artists closed out the benefit by the Opera House Association on August 27, 1883.

The very first "super star" to perform at the Grand Opera House was the great Polish actress and Countess Helena Modjeska, performing Shakespeare's comedy play, "Twelfth Night," on November 8, 1883. Her leading man, the handsome and famous Maurice Barrymore, along with his wife Georgie Drew Barrymore, also performed in the play. Maurice Barrymore and his wife Georgie Drew Barrymore were the father and mother of the famous Barrymore trio John, Lionel and Ethel.

One of the great tragedians of the stage, Lawrence Barrett, acting along with one of the greatest actors of all time, Edwin Booth, brother to actor John Wilkes Booth, gave a "one night only"(5) performance on September 28, 1887 in Shakespeare's "Julius Caesar."

An all time Oshkosh favorite comedian, John Dillon, was the first actor to perform at the Grand Opera House in the opening theater season on Saturday evening, September 1, 1883, performing the comedy play, "States Attorney."

Helena Modjeska returned on January 2, 1892, with yet another of her leading men the famous stage actor Otis Skinner, in Shakespeare's "Much Ado About Nothing."

John Philip Sousa the famous composer and conductor, dazzled "the music loving people"(6) of Oshkosh with his famous United States Marine Band on April 28, 1892, and again on March 11, 1902.

Anna Held, the great Polish born stage actress in company with impresario Florenz Ziegfeld, Jr., of the famous "Ziegfeld Follies" performed the musical comedy play,

Herrmann, Alexander (1844-1896) One of the most famous magicians ever, known as "Herrmann the Great"
Photo Courtesy of Magictricks.com

"Papa's Wife," on April 24, 1901.

The highly popular American stage actress and singer Lillian Russell, performed the racing comedy play, "Wildfire," on June 9, 1909, and the legendary Maude Adams, performed in Oshkosh on August 26, 1913 in her famous hit role success as "Peter Pan."

Great plays included the "County Fare," May 10, 1891, and "Ben Hur," on March 29, 30, and 31, 1909. Both plays used live horses that ran on special treadmills devised for the stage. "A Dark Secret," on May 8, 1891, staged dramatic "real effects" using "real boats, racing shells, and steam launches, all on a river of real water."(7)

Great magicians of the period also graced the stage of The Grand. Some of the more prominent acts included Herrmann the Great, March 27,

1895, the Great Keller, February 21, 1890, and Fredrik the Great, known later as Harry Blackstone, performed on January 9, 1916.

Russian dancer and mime Anna Pavlova, entertained audiences on December 19, 1921, while the funny and famous Four Marx Brothers, came to town on November 16, 1912.

The deaf and blind Helen Keller, "regarded as the educational wonder of the age," [8] *lectured to a large audience at The Grand on January 26, 1914.*

Footnotes: (1) The Opera House, stenograph card 1883; (2) The Opera House, stenograph card 1883; (3) The Oshkosh Daily Northwestern, Aug.6, 1883; (4) The Oshkosh Daily Northwestern, Aug.27, 1883; (5)The Daily Northwestern, Sept.28, 1887; (6) The Oshkosh Daily Northwestern, April 28, 1892; (7) The Oshkosh Times, May 5, 1891; (8) The Daily Northwestern, Jan. 27, 1914

My own recollection of the Grand in the 1950's and 60's is that it was one of several theaters in town. It was the late 1950's when the film "*Rodan*" played at The Grand. This Japanese film featured a flying prehistoric reptile that terrorized the world. By today's standard, the film would be considered a classical, even laughable Sci-Fi flick, but back in those days, it scared the daylights out of me.

In 1950, the theater was owned by Frank Bluhm and Mary Vetters. It was then The Grand Theater got its name. I recall it showing mostly B type films and second runs as The Raulf and Time Theaters had the market cornered on new releases, as the multiplex cinema's had not yet come into existence. The new owners soon changed the façade on the historic old building to give it a more modern "movie theatrical" look.

The theater had several owners, until 1969 when it was purchased by Hauser and Cook who in turn eventually leased it to two men from Rockford, Illinois. This was the bottom of the barrel for The Grand. It featured X-rated movies and the building fell into disrepair. The Grand was no longer the glorious and statuesque landmark that it once enjoyed in its early days. It had now become one of the "black eyes" of downtown and embarrassment to the city of Oshkosh.

James and Joanne Alderson are credited with launching the effort to restore The Grand and its opulence back to its origin. The "Save The Grand" movement was formed and a special committee created. Mr. James Alderson was my seventh grade teacher at Roosevelt School. He and his wife Joanne were both dedicated to theater and made it their

The Grand Theater 1964
Photo Credit: Dan Radig

life's work to save and restore The Grand to its original beauty. After 20 years of hard work and efforts to overcome financial and organizational obstacles, The Grand reached its next phase of resurrection. In 1980, a referendum was approved for the city to assume ownership, restoration and operation of the property. When the theater was built in 1883, construction costs were $36,000. In 1980, the city purchased the property for $108,500. Renovation costs upon completion are estimated at $3.1 million.

Renovation occurred through most of the 1980's and again in 2009 when ceiling structure issues were discovered. In February 2009, the Grand was closed for emergency repairs.

It is listed on the Historical Register of Historic Places (in 1974), owned by the city of Oshkosh and managed by the Oshkosh Opera House Foundation.

Today, the Opera House hosts nearly 100 public performances each year including national touring artists, educational programs, performances by the Oshkosh Community Players and Oshkosh Symphony Orchestra, as well as performances by four area high schools, regional arts groups, performances presented by independent promoters, business meetings and weddings.

***Editors Note:** **The cover** of this book features a postcard photo I discovered of the Grand Opera House at the turn of the century. The photograph above it was taken by me in 2009. I took the photograph <u>before</u> I found the postcard, so I just chose a spot that portrayed this great old landmark in all its glory. The identical positioning of both iconic images is surprising. When the postcard was made, the person would have stood right outside the Athearn Hotel. Today a bank parking lot sits where the Athearn once stood.*

The Mode

In 1939, a new theater opened in Oshkosh. The Mode was located on the corner of 12th and Oregon, directly across from the Star Theater. Memories of The Mode are a bit vague as I had only been there for a movie once or twice. I lived clear across town on the west side, and I didn't know the bus route, (if there was one) that would take us there. The other reason I seldom frequented The Mode, was it mainly ran "B" type or second run movies.

The Mode closed in 1959 and the building became a place of worship and healing by a man named AC Valdez Jr, who as it turns out is a story in itself, but not for here and now. Google the name and you will find some pretty interesting information, including involvement with a murder in Canada!

The building still is located there today, directly next to Red's Pizza and "kitty korner" from Oak's Candies.

The Oshkosh Theater and The Bijou

One of the earliest theaters in Oshkosh, The Oshkosh Theater was opened in 1927, near the end of the silent picture era. It was equipped with a powerful Barton organ. Barton Organs were made in Oshkosh

Mode Theater
Photo Credit: Ed and August Tiedje

and the organ music and audio effects were designed to make-up for the lack of sound in the silent movie. It's been reported in Michael Goc's book *Oshkosh at 150* ..."a good organist could evoke terror, romance, excitement, joy and sadness as audiences watched the silent images on the screen. Within a year, the new Strand/Raulf Hotel was built with a large theater and the first sound projection equipment in the city. Within a couple of years, all theaters in Oshkosh had sound projection.

The "100" block of Main Street then (today, the 400 block) was a hotbed of movie theaters. The Rex and Orpheum were early 20th century movie theaters along this stretch of business. A few doors down was The Bijou Theater. Opened in 1905, it was the first movie house with projection equipment and forward facing seats. One day, not long ago, I came upon a postcard from the interior of the Bijou. As this theater was gone long before I was born, I had not heard of it. I checked with several of my elders, and they had a difficult time recalling it as well. One day, I received a call from my daughter Brooke's friend "Ratch." Andy "Ratch" Ratchman works in his family business, Camera Casino on Main Street. Ratch's dad Jay Ratchman owns the business and I knew Jay from days in the National Guard as he was also a member of the 1157 Transportation Company stationed here. Ratch said, "Hey, I understand you are doing work on historical places in Oshkosh and are asking around about The Bijou Theater. C'mon down to the store, I think we've got something you'd like to see."

I drove down to Camera Casino the next day and met Ratch and Jay working in the store. I greeted Jay with a hearty handshake and we briefly reminisced about our days together in the Guard. Jay then explained "This is the location of the Bijou Theater you are interested in. There have been many businesses in this location since that day, but a previous tenant shared some history on this building that included The Bijou". Jay brought out a scrapbook of sort, and opened it up very carefully. The book contained a list of the businesses and some promotional advertisements from those businesses.

Here's what the record shows for businesses that operated in the William Hill Building at 165 Main St. starting in 1876. (Provided courtesy of Jay Ratchman)

1876-1890	William Hill & Company – Dry Goods and Carpet (The Wm Hill logo can be seen at the top front of the building in the photo below, now removed)
1893	Hough & Topliff – Carpet & Dry Goods
1895	Charles H. Shields and Company – Dry Goods and Carpet
1898	Vacant
1900-1905	Rudd & Company – Hardware, Stoves, Furniture
1905-1912	Bijou Theater
1912-1920	Majestic Theater
1920	Roy Cummings Amusement Enterprises (Majestic Theater)
1922-1924	Saxe Amusement Enterprises (Majestic Theater)
1928-1934	Vacant
1936	Lonnie's Shine Parlor & News Stand
1938	Vacant
1940-1946	National Tea Company
1949	Vacant
1951	Oshkosh War Supply
1953	Vacant

Theaters

1955-1984 Jeffrey's – Ladies Shop
1985-1986 Vacant
1987-2008 Race Office Supplies, Inc.
2008-Today Camera Casino

The Oshkosh Theater
Photo Credit: Dan Radig

Interior of Bijou Theater, Postcard

On my visit to Camera Casino that day, Jay and Andy took me upstairs to a storage area, not open or visible to the public. Not unlike many of downtowns old buildings, this one has been remodeled many times through the years. As we entered the room, I immediately could see remnants of the old theater that once stood proud there. Where we stood, I imagined, was once the balcony area. As I looked toward where the screen would have been, I could see the edges and corners of the old screen still hiding there a century later. The frame of the screen was very ornate and carved of wood. I turned to the opposite wall where the two "pigeon holes" are still visible. One hole was where the projector once shined through; the other was for the projectionist to view the screen. Andy and Jay were excited to and said they planned to explore more when time allowed.

100 Years Later...

Bijou Theater/Wm Hill Bldg
c.1908
Photo Credit: Jay Ratchman

Camera Casino/ Wm Hill Bldg
2008
Photo Credit: Randy Domer

The 44 Outdoor Theater

One of my favorite memories as a child was going to the outdoor theater. Located near the intersection of Highways 41 and 44 on the southern outskirts of town was the 44 Outdoor Theater. In the 1950's, few businesses existed "way out there". Bordered to the west, Duwe Precast Company had a concrete business nearby, and across Highway 44 toward the southeast was the Winnebago County Airport. The "Outdoor", as we always called it, was mostly surrounded by fields and highways. It was located here, far away from residential areas, so as not to disturb local residents.

The driveway into the Outdoor was located on Highway 44, about a half mile southwest of 20th Street and South Park Drive. As you pulled into the entrance off the highway, you drove up to a ticket window. The early movie-goers would line up at the ticket window until they opened. Once the admission was paid, cars could then drive on into a large, fan shaped gravel parking lot with rows of speakers on metal posts. The large outdoor screen was huge and the rows to park in formed a radius in the viewing area in front of it. The screen faced east so the setting sun did not play a factor on visibility. Each row in the gravel lot was slightly elevated so when you parked next to the speaker post, you had a slightly elevated view of the screen.

Once the perfect spot was selected, the car would maneuver back and forth to get close to the speaker stand, and just slightly ahead so the driver's side door would open. Once in position, the driver's side window would be rolled down, the metal speaker would be removed from the post and brought inside the car. The speaker was attached to the post with electrical wires that powered the speaker. Many times, late at night at the end of the movies, sleepy patrons would forget to put the speaker back in its place and drive off, pulling the speaker from its stand. A one-button volume control allowed some adjustment of the volume, which was not very good. It sounded like the voices were coming through a tin can.

In front of the screen was "playland". Early arrivals would get situated and then send the kids up front to play on the various playground toys. Swings, teeter totters and more entertained the children while mom and dad got a few moments of peace before the movies started and helped the kids burn off some of their pent up energy.

Aerial View of the 44 Outdoor Theater
Photo Credit: Richard Jungwirth

In the center of the lot sat a small brick building that housed a concession stand and restrooms. Patrons could buy everything from popcorn, peanuts and candy bars to soda pop and hot dogs.

As we entered our mid teen years and able to drive, the outdoor took on a whole new meaning. As teens, we would hide a person or two in the trunk to sneak them in without paying. Once inside, we would drive to a spot we felt was somewhat obscure and pop the trunk latch freeing our stowaway buddies. Sometimes, kids would sneak in by hiding along the edge and at dusk, jump the fence and find their friends' car to join the fun.

On weekends, it was the perfect place for a date. A boy would take his girlfriend and work up the courage to put his arm around her shoulders, waiting for the chance to steal a kiss.

"Buck Nite" was always very popular. Usually reserved for a mid week night when business was a bit slow, a whole carload could get in the gate for a dollar! Load up the station wagon and bring the whole family!

If you decided to leave early, that is, before the final movie was over, as a courtesy, you drove out of the lot with your headlights off and parking lights on. The reason for that was to ensure you did not disturb

THEATERS

A speaker system like this was used at the 44 Outdoor Theater
Photo Credit: Randy Domer

the viewing pleasure of the other patrons with your headlights. Occasionally, someone would forget and turn their headlights on by mistake. Their error was immediately brought to their attention by a chorus of beeping horns. Once you reached the gate, a sign there reminded you to turn your headlights on before exiting.

The 44 Outdoor Theater had its Grand Opening on July 15, 1949 and turned off the lights for the season the weekend of September 21-23, 1984. (Source: Cinematreasures. org) The following season, the 44 Outdoor Theater did not re-open.

Grand Opening, July 15, 1949,
Oshkosh Daily Northwestern

Final Weekend, Friday, September 21, 1984
Oshkosh Daily Northwestern

Telephones

Number please?

Telephone service in the 1950's was quite different than today. No cell phones, texting, Skype, cameras or internet service. Back then, the concept of the internet only existed in the minds of deep thinking scientists and was only a dream at that.

Telephones such as this were the style, soon to be replaced by modern technology like dials and pushbuttons

There were no dials or buttons to push. You simply lifted the receiver out of its cradle and put it to your ear. An operator would come on the line and ask "Number please?" You told her the number you wanted to call, and she would make the connection for you. There were no area codes.

Oshkosh extensions were "Blackhawk" and "Stanley". As the population grew and technology improved (dial phones were just around the corner), eventually "Beverly" was added. A telephone number then looked something like this BE5-0123 (BE abbreviated for Beverly of course).

Telephones

A staff of operators like those in this photo worked to connect every call individually

There was only one local phone company back then. Staffed with a team of operators (mostly, if not all, women) that sat at a bank of electronic boards, they would manually connect and disconnect each and every call.

For long distance calls, you would lift the receiver, the operator would come on the line and say "number please", and you would say "long distance please". The local operator would then connect you to a long distance operator who would take the information from you, then connect you.

If you wanted to save a little money, you could sign up for a "Party Line". A party line meant you shared phone service with another person, usually a neighbor. If you lifted up the phone while the other party was talking, you could listen to their entire conversation. Constant interruptions were common as you kept checking to see if the other person had finished.

Our phones didn't take photos, have keypads to send text messages, download music or give you radar weather or even the time of day. The phone company however DID have a free service in which you dialed a number and a recorded announcement gave you the time.

Our phones didn't have maps or step by step driving directions, or help you find the nearest gas station or restaurant. And they weren't cordless; you were tethered to the wall or plug in phone jack.

It just made phone calls…exactly like Alexander Graham Bell intended!

Garlic Island

One of the geographic features of Oshkosh that drew settlers and Native Americans to this area was the bountiful waters that surround our great city. Lake Butte des Morts to the west narrows down to the Fox River which winds its way through town before meeting the shores of Lake Winnebago to our east.

As you travel the area waterways and follow the navigational route toward the cities of Neenah, Menasha and Appleton, you will pass by a beautiful island located just a mile or two north of the city limits.

Welcome to Garlic Island!

As a boy, I spent many summers at the cottage of my Uncle Neil and Aunt Loretta Ziebell, whose property is located on Island View Drive, just a couple hundred yards from the island, affording a breath taking view. My cousin Lee and I would wonder what it would be like to paddle our little plastic boat over to the island and explore. A few times we set off to do just that, only to be called back by my aunt "You kids are going to drown in that thing! Get back here right now." Not wearing any life vests, she was probably right. But at eight years old, what did we know?

Not much was ever said about the history of Garlic Island, in fact, I doubt many people in Oshkosh even knew it existed unless they fished or boated Lake Winnebago.

Here's a little history on one of my favorite places. Much of this information was provided by Wally Bergstrom, whose family now own the island, neighbor and local historian Dan Reinhold, the Radford Family and my cousin, Dianne (Ziebell) Senderhauf, who worked at the Public Library before recently retiring.

(1) During the War of 1812, before Wisconsin reached statehood, the island was occupied by British soldiers. The winter of 1813-14 was a bitter one. The Menominee and Winnebago Indians here became

dependent upon the British for their supplies and supply lines were disrupted by the extreme conditions. In his journal, Col. Robert Dickson writes: (1) *"I am heartily sick and tired of this place. There is no situation more miserable than to see objects around you dying with hunger, and unable to give them but little assistance. I have done what I could for them, and will in consequence starve myself."* Later, he writes *"I can hardly hold my pen for the cold."* Col. Dickson and his troops worked hard to keep the allegiance with the Indians. On Christmas Day, 1813, Dickson notes *"I hear nothing but the cry of hunger from all quarters."* By February 4, 1814, they ran out of provisions. The situation looked grim when two days later, supplies arrived from the post in Green Bay. By April, the British encampment moved on to Mackinac. *(1) ref: Wisconsin Magazine of History, 1962)*

Over the years, the island has known many names. Formerly known as *Island Park, Radford Island and The Island,* Garlic *(and Garlick) Island* has been privately owned for over a century. Ownership today (2012) belongs to the Bergstrom Family. In a May 26, 1970 article, Oshkosh newspaper "The Paper" reported the island to be owned by Lynn Werner, president of the Neenah based Werner Electric Supply Company and the Keil & Werner Electric Company. The Werner and Buckstaff families were good friends and when Lynn Werner died in 1984, the Bergstrom family purchased the island and adjoining properties on Perkins Point from the Werner estate.

Family friends recall when Lynn passed away. "Lynn's request was to be cremated and his ashes scattered about the island." The family honored that request and did as Mr. Werner had instructed. "That was quite a day. When the ashes were scattered, a little extra was put in and around the duck blinds. Lynn was an avid hunter and one of his favorite pastimes was duck hunting on his beloved Garlic Island."

Early records indicate the first owner to be a friend of Governor Doty, Judge Morgan Martin in 1840 with a land grant from the US Government. On February 1, 1843, the island and a small piece of land on the shore of Island Point was sold to Ann Smith. According to research done by the Oshkosh Public Museum in 2009, it is believed Smith intended to farm this area.

In 1868, William Ihrig of Oshkosh purchased the land from Smith. He, too, had the intent of growing corn and grain on the fertile soil on the mainland. He and his family farmed this area for 8 years until he suffered financial difficulties and poor health.

In 1877 the property was acquired by the Island Park Association, a stock company comprised originally of 20 members of the Oshkosh Yacht Club, as a rendezvous point for the organization's cruises and outings. (Source: View Magazine, Oct. 31, 1976) This group was known as the Island Park Association. Each member made an initial contribution of $100 each which was used to build a hotel with 12 rooms and 11 small cottages. The island was kept open to the public and newspaper ads in the Chicago area highlighting the tremendous paradise in the wilds of Wisconsin. It is said the resort was very busy in the summer but financially unsuccessful. A newspaper article from June 10, 1881 describes an annual excursion of stockholders of Island Park. *"There was quite a large party of stockholders and others on board the steamer Carter. The boat also carried a tame fawn presented to the association by Adam Bell, which will hereafter make it's home on the island. K.M. Hutchinson also took along some seabright bantams (tame fofwl) as a donation to the zoological attractions to the island. The latter are for the exclusive purpose of catching bugs."*

In 1889, a fire from the stovepipe on the cook stove burned the hotel to the ground. Reports indicated the building burned in less than 15 minutes. Valued at $2,000, it was uninsured. At a meeting later that summer, the Island Park Association decided not to rebuild the hotel and put the island up for sale.

Fall of 1889 saw new ownership take over the property and formed the Island Park Company. This group consisted of 19 well-to-do men from the Oshkosh area – some of which were the lumber barons of that time – Morgan, Warwick, Sawyer, C. Radford, Kimberly, Thompson and Smith. Other notable investors included Andrew Jackson and George W. Gates. It was their intent to "build a summer home community for their families to enjoy all the benefits that their Eastern counterparts enjoyed in their vacation areas.

The island was surveyed into 28 lots, and the owners drew straws for placement. 17 of the owners built homes over the following 3 ½ years. A common dining hall was built and used for education of their children and a dance hall for evening entertainment. The dance hall was located on Lot #1 on the southwest corner of the island. (Editor's Note: In 1931, this building was sold to the Town of Oshkosh and moved across the ice. The Town used it as their town hall for a number of years. The building now is owned by Struensee, Inc. and still today stands on the edge of County A near Sherman Road.)

This group being better financed than the previous one, contracted with the steamboat named the *Mayflower* to transport guests to and from the city's Main Street bridge platform. The ship was 84 ft long and made two trips daily to the island. Through the years, various steamships were used to transport guests to the island. They seemed to change for various reasons including availability and change of ownership.

On August 10, 1901, Stephan Radford, whose brother Charles was one of the original investors in the Island Park Association, gained his first ownership on the island when he received an assignment of Lot 6 formerly owned by George Bowman. In that same late summer of 1901, Stephan Radford began buying up the leases from other property owners. Records indicate some transactions were simple, but others, where there were estates involved, required much correspondence and litigation. Some lots had been repossessed for non-payment of assessments, so they then belonged to the Island Company.

Over the next eight years, Radford had bought up most of the leases and with his family, lived for many summers on the island. Winnebago County historian George Nevitt and close friend of Radford, says the owner bred championship white collie dogs on the island, and one of the dogs was presented to President Calvin Coolidge as a gift. At one time, Radford planted an apple orchard and more than a half acre of daffodils there.

In 1931, several years after Radford's death, the island was purchased by three incorporators of Island Point, Inc. Attorneys Charles Williams and J. C. Thompson with businessman Clyde Terrell owned the property until selling it to Lynn Werner in 1948.

Christy's Portrait of Mrs. Coolidge with Radford's White Collie

Legend tells us the name Garlic Island derived from the plants growing wild on the island at one time. Settlers allegedly mistook the leek plants for garlic.

As mentioned earlier, *The Island* was sponsored by the Oshkosh Yacht Club for the amusement for the upper classes and included excursions in private motorized yachts and sailing regattas.

A travel brochure from that era describes The Island as follows (source: Oshkosh Public Library 977.564/917.7564; I822 cop.1):

THE ISLAND

The Island has no hotel, but eleven excellent cottages (without kitchens) and a central dining hall, besides a large pavilion and an office. The cottages are all constructed so that those desiring one or two rooms can be accommodated as easily as those wishing a whole cottage. Each cottage has a large sitting room for common use. These conditions naturally make The Island a homelike, quiet and restful place, entirely unlike the ordinary hotel resort. The size is such that one always realizes it is an island.

THE TRUTH

It is desirable to state in the beginning that in the careful compiling of this book, not one statement has been allowed to enter that is not founded on absolute fact, and that the chief and foremost thing concerning this advertisement is it's truth. A Unique Feature – The charge for boarding is the beginning and end of all expense at The Island. There Are No Extras – Transportation of guests and baggage from the city dock is free. Riders on The Island launch at any time are free. Row boats are free. The large Island sailboat is at the free disposal of guests. No feeing is expected or desired.

DESCRIPTION

The Island is eleven acres in area. The soil is porous, so the ground becomes dry almost directly after a heavy rain. It is high and well drained, with no marshy places. The vegetation is no-where of an obnoxious character and the tall ancient elm trees afford a comfortable shade. There is never a day without it's (sic) cool breeze, and although but a few minutes rowing distance from mainland, the temperature is several degrees lower on the Island. The west shore forms a perfect harbor for all boats in all weathers.

COTTAGES

It is difficult to explain to correspondents how radically different the cottages on The Island are from the usual resort cottages. They have to be seen to be appreciated. They were built at considerable expense for private summer homes. Every cottage picture in this book is an exact photographic reproduction of an Island cottage. All have large sitting rooms and fireplaces. All have toilet rooms and closets. All have wide porches running across front and back, and in some instances, entirely around. Many of the chambers are of sufficient size to accommodate an entire family. In almost every case, the furnishings were purchased with cottages; so all are homelike and comfortable.

FAMILIES

People with small children will find The Island an unusually attractive place. Families can be made truly comfortable in the large airy cottages, with plenty of closet room. Three of the largest cottages will accommodate with comfort twelve people. A rate is made for all families staying any length of time and for small children.

CHILDREN

A distinctive feature of The Island is it's appropriativeness for children. The beach around the harbor, free boat rides to the city, and every outdoor amusement at hand to keep them busy, healthy and happy. The water is shallow all along the shore-line, making a safe play-ground of the beach.

HEALTH

The Island holds a local reputation for being the healthiest spot on the lake. As has been said before, it is high, the soil exceedingly dry, and drainage of the best. The water served at the table comes from a deep artesian well on the island. Arrangements have been made to secure milk fresh twice daily from nearby farmers. For families with children, let it be said, that no healthier, safer place can be found.

LAKE WINNEBAGO

For years, this magnificent sheet of water has been neglected. Now interest is being taken, an as it's great size (thirty by twelve miles) makes it particularly fine for yachting, it will probably soon become the most popular lake in the Northwest. The broad expanse of water serves to cool the surrounding air, and makes the lake unusually safe, for storms can always be seen approaching for some time before they break. Whether one wishes to row, sail, fish, swim or ride on a steamer, this lake cannot be surpassed.

TRANSPORTATION

During July and August a launch will make two daily trips to The Island from Main Street dock, Oshkosh. In June and September, the boat will run as required. The dock is only ten minutes walk from any railway passenger station in the city. There will be no charge on the boat for either passengers or baggage. Guests are welcome to take the lake rides at anytime. *This unusual feature should be borne in mind when rates are considered.*

BOATING

The pleasure of rowing can be safely indulged in by all ages during the day or evening. Boats are free and the harbor offers a good time to children, for there they can learn to row within sight of their parents.

THE WOODEN SHOE

This fishing shack was purchased for the pleasure of The Island guests, and on fine evenings it takes all who care to go for a sail. It is one of those large, wide, deep, safe craft, built for all kinds of weather. Old and young feel comfortable and secure about going, for when the "Wooden Shoe" takes out the islanders, there will be none but a careful and experienced sailor in charge. Private boats of any size or kind will be cared for.

TENNIS

There is a fine, level court laid out in the center of the Island. As there is always a lake breeze, the sport can be enjoyed every day of the summer. Quoits, croquet, basket-ball and bolo are also provided for.

PAVILLION

The dancing pavilion is admirably arranged for a good time. A piano is provided, and the guests have entire freedom of the place at all times. It is close to the water, and the veranda is a delightfully cool spot. Being situated some distance from the cottages, the pleasure of the young people will not disturb those desiring rest and quiet. The smooth hardwood floor makes dancing an especial pleasure.

The Island launch makes two trips daily from Main Street dock, Oshkosh—10:00 am and 5:00 pm. Guests arriving on the 5:10 train can have the boat held for them if due notice is given.

Rates are based on the number in a family, rooms required, and length of stay. Very reasonable terms will be quoted families remaining a month or more.

The Island Co.,
Oshkosh, Wis.

The October 31, 1976 issue of *View Magazine* reports:

"At one time...there were upwards of 500 elm trees on the island, besides many old bass woods. The raising of the waters of the lake, by reason of the Neenah and Menasha damns has greatly reduced the size of the island. Many of its finest trees have been carried away by high water and ice. The original name Garlic Island was replaced by resort owners who felt the name wasn't very conducive to resort life."

As legends have it, this one is my favorite. I enjoy telling this story to my grandchildren who look at me kind of strange and wonder if I'm pulling their leg.

I draw my credibility with this story to a report published in The Oshkosh Daily Northwestern, the year is uncertain. Northwestern reporter Carl Hinz wrote an article on the legend of the Indian Princess.

Carl writes : *Many years ago-according to the legend-at a time then already age shrouded in Indian memory, there dwelt on an island at the foot of the lake, an old chieftain and his only daughter, Wau-we-te (Spirit Queen).*

This old chief was deeply revered by his people for the profound sagacity he evidenced in his leadership of them.

Although his tribesmen abided on the mainland shore, the ancient sage was ever insistent upon remaining with his daughter alone on his island and never allowed any of his followers to set foot upon its shores.

At each new moon he would guide his bark canoe to the mainland and at night, before the council fire, with the village old men gathered around him, would reveal to them the mandates of the almighty Manitou (God) as these had been imparted to him during his nightly vigils at his island home.

Never, on these occasions had he brought with him his daughter, Wau-we-te. No other eyes but his have beheld her charms. Save for the old fellow's occasional allusions to her sagacity and loveliness, absolutely nothing was known of her among the tribesmen. Her very existence might have been a figment of his visionary dreams and so she soon came to be regarded as a sort of semi-mortal wood nymph-a mysterious spirit, who perhaps exercised some potent influence on their destiny. Strange tales were whispered about concerning her, especially among the women of the tribe. There were many of the opinion that she was in reality the old man's daughter that he had plighted her to be the bride of the mighty Manitou and it was for this reason that no one was ever permitted to behold her. Others believed that she was a strange wild creature who consorted with the wood gods and that the butterflies were her children.

After many moons of prosperity and plenty had passed on in the eternal cycle of the seasons, the old man's life was ebbing to its close.

The season was Indian Summer Time. Glistening mists floated over the lake and the trees on the shore were draped with gleaming frost fronds. It is a time particularly potent with religious significance. Early one morning, the old man rose and looked over the lake. He saw the pale gold of first dawn spilling its sheen on the morning mist veiled water. As the blazing face of the sun emerged from beyond the eastern horizon and suffused the whole surface of the lake in its crimson splendor, he believed he beheld reflected in the water the face of mighty Manitou, who then appeared before him and in mighty accents spoke to him. The old chief knew then that his time had come to journey to the happy hunting ground of his people.

On the opposite shore, sentinel braves, their keen eyes piercing the haze of the morning mist, could dimly discern smoke signals issuing from the island of their chief. These were interpreted as a summons for the wise men of the tribe to journey to the island. And so, for the first time, the tribesmen set foot on the mysterious island and for the first time beheld the beautiful princess Wau-we-te.

The tribal sages gathered around their chief as the old man imparted to them his last words of wisdom. When the sun had passed into darkness, he said, his spirit would leave him and journey to the hereafter land. He also predicted when the sun had three times passed into darkness, a horde of evil spirits would come from the southland and attempt to carry off Wau-we-te. Might Manitou, however, would destroy them and Wau-we te would be left to rule in his stead. This, he said, was the message of Manitou.

When the shadows of dusk had driven the sun westward to be engulfed by the shades of night, the old chief died and so the first of his prophetic utterances had materialized.

After the sun had three times more repeated its blazing course through the heavens came the promised invasion. However, Wau-we-te forewarned by her father's prophecy had already departed from her island home and so was not apprehended. And, as fore-ordained, mighty Manitou sent a terrific tempest which lashed the waters of the lake into a turbulent frenzy. Thunder roared as countless thrusts of livid lightning pierced the darkness and struck here and there-in a hundred places in the thrashing water and on the wave lashed shore. Only the camping grounds of the Indians was excepted from this elemental onslaught.

When the next day broke bright and clear, no vestige of the island remained. It, together with its invaders, had been completely engulfed in the waters of Winnebago. It was then Wau-we-te revealed to her tribe that Manitou had appeared to her on the preceding night and instructed her to lead her people northward along the shore of the lake where she would find her island for he had lifted it out of the water and carried it away to be *deposited in this safer location where it would remain forever secure from invasion.*

Here, for many moons dwelt the Queen and people in security and peace. Like her father, Wau-we-te ruled her tribe with sagacity and gentleness so no strife or avarice were known to them. Though many braves sought her favor, legend has it that she remained unwedded until the end of her days for she was the earthly consort of the great Manitou.

For many generations after her demise,, offerings were brought to her grave on the island in propitiation of her memory and the place was called "Island of God" by the Indians. It is related that after her death, hatred, avarice, selfishness and war came into the world.

I believe it to be true.

Today, I enjoy each morning as I wake and look out the window of my bedroom at the peaceful solitude of Garlic Island. Ducks and geese abound in the Fall. In summer, the island is home to nesting pairs of Pelicans and Cormorants who battle the local seagulls for the fish that are so plentiful these days. At night, the moonlight dances like diamonds across the water.

It's just the way Wau-we-te would want it.

Garlic Island today

Winnebago County Airport

As the city of Oshkosh grew, it started to attract new business. Located in the heart of the Fox Valley, the airport in Oshkosh was a popular hub for travelers coming to conduct business with Oshkosh Truck, American Can, Kimberly Clark and many other key valley businesses.

Winnebago County Airport (now Wittman Field) is located on the south edge of 20th Street. The runways covered a good portion of the land that is now home to the EAA. Runway lengths were adequate for commercial airlines then. The most prominent carrier was North Central Airlines.

North Central Airlines was a Minneapolis based airline that was founded in Clintonville, WI in 1944 as Wisconsin Central Airlines. Eventually, through various acquisitions and mergers, it became Northwest Airlines based in Minneapolis in 1986 and has since merged with Delta Airlines.

As small as it was, Winnebago County Airport thrived in the 1960's. The terminal building was a small brick building that contained a passenger waiting area, adjacent to a wonderful little café called Mike's Grill owned and operated by Oshkosh businessman Mike Goerlitz. Three car rental companies manned counters to serve passengers needing transportation. Avis, National and Hertz (whom I worked for at one time) provided car rentals while a local limousine service greeted passengers that only wanted taxi type service. The Hertz job was a second job that served to subsidize my meat cutting job. We were young, newly married and our family was starting to grow. We did what we needed to support our family, so three weeknights and the occasional Sunday were the norm. I wore the Hertz bright yellow blazer and company standard black and yellow striped tie. My job was to greet each flight and accommodate reservations with a clean new car. In between flights, I was required to service returned vehicles which included running them through the car wash and see that the interiors were vacuumed and free of any debris. That included emptying the ashtrays as most everyone smoked in those days. A spritz of "auto freshener" and the rental was ready to go!

Usually I brought my lunch, or Karen would bring me a hot dinner, but on a rare occasion I would walk to Mike's Grill between flights and sit at the counter and order a sandwich. Karen Fisher, a former high school classmate, was the waitress there. This was a very popular spot for local police and sheriff's deputies. The hot beef sandwich with gravy and mashed potatoes was the best!

Winnebago County Airport 1959
Photo Credit: Dan Radig

On June 29, 1972 a terrible tragedy happened over the waters of Lake Winnebago, just north of Oshkosh. At 10:37am, a North Central Airlines Convair CV 580, Flight 290, collided midair with an Air Wisconsin Twin Otter aircraft. The accident description was listed by the FAA as failure by both aircrafts to see and avoid the other. The mid-air crash made national news that evening. The entire city sat in front of their television sets as Walter Cronkite reported the terrible news.

Along the shore of Lake Winnebago, near the crash site, by standers watched in horror and awe as pieces of the wreckage were pulled from the depths of the lake and taken by barge to an empty property along the Fox River in Oshkosh, near the south end of Bowen Street. It was here that the FAA would try to sort things out and determine the cause of the accident.

The June 30, 1972 Oshkosh Daily Northwestern reported: " *The North Central Airlines plane took off from Green Bay at 10:32 am en route to Oshkosh, and the Air Wisconsin plane, a DeHavilland "Otter," a turbo-prop plane, departed Sheboygan en route for Outagamie Airport at 10:10 am. Both planes were late. The Air Wisconsin plane was about 10 minutes late for its scheduled 10:25 a.m. landing while the North Central plane, a Convair 580, was held up at Austin Straubel Field in Green Bay for about two hours. Officials from North Central said the reason for the delay was "technical." They blamed a lack of coordination between the arrival of baggage, crew and passengers for the delay. Boyer said the North Central plane was entering into its approach landing path and was almost set for confirmation of landing at Wittman Field when the crash occurred. ... The North Central plane had a total capacity of 48 persons while the Canadian-built Air Wisconsin craft could carry a total of 15, officials said. Lost were two passengers and a crew of three in the North Central plane and two crew members and six passengers in the Air Wisconsin aircraft.*

Officials Thursday afternoon found only one body and parts of others that floated to the top near the crash scene. Officials said the airplanes crashed about 1 ½ to 2 miles east of Limekiln Road in Neenah south of the Neenah Point. Many eyewitnesses, sunning themselves in 80 degree weather near the Neenah Pool at Recreation Park on South Park Avenue saw the explosion as well as other cottage owners and other park-goers who were at Doty Park, disembarkment point for recovery boats...Both planes were flying in very good VFR (Visual Flight Rule) condition...cloud formations were at 3,000 feet and scattered, and at 15,000 feet the cloud formations were thinly broken. Visibility was five miles and officials said the clear blue sky was filled with a haze which may have hampered visual sighting by either craft...Following the crash, Neenah police were contacted first. Reports stated that 11-year-old Robert Pitts Jr, 860 Paynes Point Beach Road, Neenah saw the crash and reported it to his mother, who called police at 10:31 am. The Pitts boy and a friend, Gregg Johnson, 10, were canoeing on the lake when they observed an explosion in the air."

In the same Oshkosh Daily Northwestern edition, another article reports:

Crash Results In Mail Delay
Some business and residential mail for the Oshkosh sectional area will be delayed after being recovered from Lake Winnebago at the scene of the crash of a North Central Airlines plane. Postmaster Clarence Spalding said that a postal inspector had received six pouches of mall, containing about 3,000 pieces, from the scene of the accident, destined for Oshkosh from the Minneapolis office. The mail was being dried out today at the post office to make it deliverable, and it is expected all of it will reach destinations by Saturday, the postmaster said.

Thirteen people lost their lives that day. There were no survivors. As stated in the Oshkosh Daily Northwestern's report, the captain and pilot of the Air Wisconsin plane was David Jacobs. "Jake" was a fellow National Guardsman in my unit, the 1157 Transportation Company in Oshkosh.

The Pizza Parlor

Oshkosh has always had a reputation for good pizza, and it was no different in the 50's and 60's. Most pizza parlors offered inside seating which made them very popular for teenagers especially on Friday night after a Rec Dance, YMCA Dance or South Park Dance.

My earliest memories of Oshkosh pizza start with Jess and Nick's. Jess and Nick's was located on Main, next to Wussow's Steak House near the "Rocket Corner" (Main and Irving). The "Rocket Corner was named so because of the car dealership located there. Badger Oldsmobile was one of the largest car dealerships in town, and on the roof of the building was a Rocket symbolizing the Oldsmobile Rocket 88, which of course was powered by the 394 cubic inch Rocket V-8 engine.

Jess and Nicks started in the pizza business in 1954. Jess Jones and Nicholas Connelly were partners and were one of the very first businesses to cash in on the fast growing popularity of pizza. As the story goes, after World War II, servicemen returned home and wanted the pizza they had tried in Europe. Americans' love for this delicious Italian dish actually started on the east coast in New York City and after a few years spread across the USA.

I remember my Dad working for Jess and Nick's in the evening as a part time delivery guy, after driving a truck all day long. Sometimes, my dad would stop by the house, usually later in the evening, with an extra pizza. This would happen when someone would call up and order a pizza to an address which they were playing a prank. Dad would go up, knock on the door and then would get turned away. "We didn't order a pizza!" So Dad would drop it off at our house and boy were we always glad when he did! Pizza was a treat we didn't get often in the early days of our family. My dad also moonlighted as a sign painter and he was quite good. He painted most of the pizza delivery vans in town, including Jess and Nick's, Red's, and West End to name a few.

Jess and Nick's was one of the most popular pizza places in the 50's and 60's, delivering hot, fresh pizza to your door or at your table in their dining area. Jess and Nick were only in business together for about a year, and then Jess and his brother Warren joined ranks to keep the business going. They moved from 703 N. Main Street to 566 Main Street around 1960. The larger building provided more dining area and better suited the overall business needs. They served hot, fresh pizza until 1966, and then Jess Jones tried to move his business away from dining room and delivery to the fresh and frozen pizza format. He had only some limited success for a few years, eventually going out of business.

West End Pizza got their start around this same time. John Neustifter was a local butcher and knew Red Lawler who worked out at the State Hospital in the food service area. On October 27, 1958, these two

> **OPENING**
>
> FRIDAY, FEB. 3rd
> AT 4 P. M.
>
> THE NEW
>
> **WEST END PIZZA**
>
> For Home Delivery
> PHONE BE. 5-6650
>
> 111 N. Sawyer St.
> Oshkosh
>
> CLOSED ON MONDAYS

Oshkosh Daily Northwestern Ad from Feb. 1, 1961

guys teamed up with third partner and opened a pizza business at 711 Oregon Street, cleverly named "The Pizza Parlor".

This was the beginning of what would become two of the most successful pizza venues in Oshkosh. According to Jeff "Blackie" Weigandt, current owner of West End Pizza and grandson to John Neustifter, "These guys were friends, even after they decided to go their own direction". Not unlike many business partnerships, John and Red had their own ideas on where they saw their business going.

On February 3, 1961, Neustifter opened his own business. The West End Pizza Palace was located at 111 N. Sawyer Street, next door to Nubs and Leroy's Service Station and across the street from Lourdes High School.

John R. Neustifter, affectionately known as "Schnockeye", quickly built a reputation for one of the best pizza's in town. "My Grandpa had a reputation for tipping a few" Blackie said with a chuckle. "I guess that's where he got the nickname". The name was famous on the west side of town. In fact, people would commonly comment, "Let's order a pizza from Schnockeyes!"

The reputation for the best pizza didn't come easy or by chance. "Being a butcher by trade, my grandfather would buy his meat fresh, bone it out, and grind the trimmings into sausage. The seasoning he used is an old family recipe, a well guarded secret that is still used today"

Weigandt said. West End still follows "Schnockeye's" standard of making their sauce and mixing and rolling their dough using only scratch ingredients.

By this time the pizza business was booming! "The phone would ring off the wall with orders, it was hard to keep up" said Blackie. Additionally, the inside dining area had room for only four tables and a juke box. Business was growing fast and they needed more room. So in 1971, West End Pizza moved from their Sawyer Street location to the NW corner of 9th Street and Knapp.

Eventually, due to age and health problems, Neustifter turned the operation of his business over to his son, John Jr. (1974-1977); then sold it in 1978 to his daughter and her husband, Annabelle and Jimmy Weigandt.

The Weigandts took things over and kept the business going. Blackie recalls "I helped my grandfather through the years so when mom and dad took over, I continued to help them when I could".

In 1983, Jeff Weigandt purchased the business from his parents and explained, "Dad and Mom wanted to spend more time in Florida so the timing was right for them to retire."

Business continued to grow and Weigandt had to make a big business decision. Inside seating was once again becoming an issue and parking on this busy intersection was extremely limited. "Also, I was closing on 50 years old and needed to decide what the future would be for the business and my family" he said. The Weigandt's had a family meeting and the kids were asked if they were interested in taking over the business someday. The indication was positive, so Blackie started looking into a site to build a larger restaurant.

On July 1, 1999 West End Pizza moved into their new and current location on 2oth Street near South Park Ave. The business is now being managed by his three sons, Ben, Aaron and Jon while Blackie spends a little more time on the golf course.

Through the years the pizza business has changed. Many chains are now here that weren't decades ago. Companies like Papa John's and Papa Murphy's along with every other tavern in town that sells a pizza, continue to compete for their share of the pizza market.

Today, the Weigandt boys are the fourth generation of the family in the pizza business. They continue to cherish family tradition and still thrive to make the best pizza in town.

Another of Oshkosh's long standing pizza traditions is Red's Pizza, still serving delicious pizza at 1123 Oregon Street. As mentioned earlier, Charles Lawler, commonly known as "Red", was partners with John Neustifter, then Lee Bradke in a business called The Pizza Parlor at 711 Oregon Street until 1962. Neustifter had already moved on forming his own business at West End, when Red decided to open his own business. It was then Red's partnership with Bradke was dissolved and he moved into the building that formerly housed The Star Theater at 1128 Oregon St. It was available for rent, so Red moved in and opened his own business as Red's Pizza. With seven children at home to care for, Red and his wife, Dorothy, were highly motivated business partners. Most of the staff from The Pizza Parlor followed Red to his new location. Bradke continued to do business as The Pizza House until 1966, and then closed.

Red's business was mainly pizza, but because of his food service background at the State Hospital and his experience as Mess Sergeant in the Oshkosh unit of the Wisconsin National Guard, Red expanded his menu to include things like sandwiches and broasted chicken. Red's son, Steve Lawler, recalls "The hamburgers were a big thing with the college kids. They'd come in here in droves for burgers and our homemade french fries!"

Red's idea to get into the pizza business started a few years earlier when Red was at Annual Training at Camp McCoy for the National Guard. "Dad, was in charge of the mess section and one night the troops were hungry, so Red looked around the kitchen area and found some leftover flour, sauce, spices, meat and other ingredients he thought would make a great pizza. So he put it all together and served it to hungry masses at the company party that evening. "The guys loved it!" Steve recalled. "They were all telling him he should go into business selling pizza!" So he did just that.

In 1968, business was booming and across the street was a restaurant that was closing. Wirtz's Fine Foods was vacating a building that was already setup as a restaurant which was just what Lawler was looking for. The business moved across the street to 1123 Oregon, where it remains today.

Red's son Steve was brought into the pizza business at an early age. "I started working with my dad when I was twelve years old" Steve said with a smile. "My first jobs included blanching our homemade French

Fries and working on the grill a little bit" he said as he admitted things were done a little differently back then. As he continued to reflect on those early years Steve recalled, "I made my first pizza when I was fourteen. Steve Lurvey worked in the kitchen and was one of our delivery guys…he taught me."

I knew Red from my days in the National Guard. Steve Lawler was in my unit so we were fellow guardsmen. Red would come to the Armory on occasion to cater a special party or just visit the guys. Red was one of the nicest, friendliest people you ever want to meet. He would give of himself to others whether he knew them or not. Steve shared a great example of his kindness and generosity.

"One year, on Christmas Eve, Red's was closing like every other business in town. He gave the "beatcop" that walked Oregon Street a key to the restaurant and told him to let himself in and make some coffee to stay warm. When the "beatcop" arrived later that Christmas Eve and let himself in, he found a big box of doughnuts…compliments of Red." Steve looked at me proudly and said, "That was my Dad"

In 1972, Red and Dorothy decided to get away from it all and moved to Wautoma. Stevie had things in Oshkosh well in hand so he thought it may be time to step back just a little from the work load. But that didn't last long. In 1974 Red decided to open a second Red's Pizza in Wautoma. That business lasted about five years before it once again became too much for the aging Red and Dorothy and the Wautoma location was closed.

In 1979, Steve Lawler bought the business from his parents and continues to serve the same delicious food with the recipes his family developed so many years ago.

Charles "Red" Lawler was born in Omro, Wisconsin in 1917 and died in 2005 at the age of 88.

Several other Pizza joints came on the scene and then one by one disappeared over time. Louarti's at 667 N. Main St. served good pizza and had a large dining room that seated many patrons. They began in business in 1962 and served patrons in that same location until 1972. After that, the business name was changed to Villa Capri and closed after one year.

The Red and Blue Lanterns had locations on Main and Irving Streets and catered more to the younger weekend crowds. After a dance or at bar time, it would be nearly impossible to get into either of the "Lantern" locations without a long line and wait. You see, most pizza parlors then did not serve alcohol so they stayed open late…until 3 or 4 am. The locations at 701 N. Main St. and 700 Jackson St. were opened by David Kitzman (owner of Mars Drive-In) in 1966. Both locations operated until 1974 by Mars Family Restaurants with the Main Street business becoming Mabel Murphy's and the property on Jackson St. listed as vacant. The Mars Family Restaurants Company also opened a Red Lantern at 539 Pearl St. from 1971-73

Pizza parlors have not disappeared since then, but they have changed. The clientele is mostly families or couples having dinner. The era of the teenage hangout has pretty much gone the way of '57 Chevy's, Beatle Boots and cruising up and down Algoma and High Streets on Friday night.

Ice Skating

In the 1950's, winters seemed to last longer than today. Perhaps this can be attributed to the fact as kids we looked forward to winters back then, and dread them as adults today. Winter meant many things to me as a child growing up in Oshkosh. The first snowfall was always very exciting. It held the promise of building snow forts, snowball fights, making snowmen and snow angels, and even the chance to make a dollar or two shoveling the neighbors' sidewalk.

The Ice Rink Between Leon's and Sno Cap Was Very Popular
Photo Credit: Ed and August Tiedje, Dan Radig

Some of the neighborhood kids who lived further north on Lark Street would often go to Sawyer Creek and skate until the snow cover ruined good skating conditions. This was always a dangerous activity, as we were usually unsure how much ice there was, especially in early winter as the ice was beginning to cover the creek. Additionally, there was a current running under the ice in some areas, which meant ice thickness would vary.

Many of the Oshkosh Public Schools had skating rinks. Roosevelt School on Sawyer Street was my school from elementary all the way through ninth grade. Each winter, a rink would be plowed on the playground located on the east side of the school. At 10 years old, it seemed enormous! Giant floodlights on top of the building illuminated the rink which was banked with snow as volunteer workers would shovel after every snowfall. Music was broadcast over the intercom system to add to our skating enjoyment. I don't know why I recall this, but the song I remember played most often was "Love Potion Number 9".

Kids of all ages from the surrounding neighborhood would arrive each evening after supper to skate. We'd form long lines and play crack the whip! I remember hoping that some of the girls I had crushes on would show up and sometimes they did. We would chase them around the rink or try to impress them with our amateur skating skills that usually ended up with us on our behind on the ice. Another fun event was rounding up as many skaters as we could to hold hands in one long line. Appropriately named "Crack the Whip", the line would start skating and build up speed. When the front skater felt we were going fast enough, he or she would make a sharp turn, quickly accelerating those at the rear of the line who usually ended up in a snow bank or sliding belly first across the rink.

A warming house was created on the north side of the building in a corridor that connected the east and west wings of the school, and alongside the gymnasium. Chaperones, who usually consisted of our school custodians or a neighbor volunteer, would sit in the warming house to supervise. A rubber mat was laid down atop the marble floors so you could walk on tip toe to the wooden benches to warm up before going out for another round. It seemed like our toes were always the first thing to get cold, in spite of the three pairs of wool socks we had on.

Each evening around 9 o'clock, the rink would close and they'd send everybody home. The custodians then pulled out the long rubber hoses and began flooding the rink. As the water froze, a new clear sheet of pristine ice was ready for the next nights skate.

Over time, the school ice rinks slowly disappeared. It might have been due to budgeting cuts…or perhaps liability issues …who knows. It is just another of those fun and simple things we did back then, that are no longer here today.

Readin', Writin' and 'Rithmetic

Growing up on Oshkosh's west side meant one thing when you were a kid. Unless your parents paid to have you attend a private or parochial school, you went to Roosevelt School.

Located on Sawyer Street between Coolidge and Tyler Avenues, Roosevelt School provided education for grades kindergarten through 9th grade in the 50's and 60's.

I entered kindergarten in the fall of 1956. Mrs. Hansen was my teacher and I attended the PM session. As is the case with most of us, my recollection of Kindergarten is a bit vague. The room, as I remember it, seemed very large. You entered the school from the Coolidge Ave side of the building, closest to the front side facing Sawyer Street. My class room was the first room to the right when entering the building. An extended room adjacent to this provided additional space for indoor activities. This adjacent room can be seen today as it juts out toward the south. In the days when I was there, that room was lined on all three sides with windows. It was bright and sunny, and great area for Kindergarten games and learning. Today the windows have been enclosed, I would speculate to save energy.

As we were in the PM session, we had a designated time for a nap in the afternoon. Each student was required to bring a throw rug from home that would be laid out on the floor at naptime, as Mrs. Hansen drew the shades and darkened the room. I'm not sure anyone ever slept, but it did provide some quiet time for a brief period, I'm sure Mrs. Hansen appreciated it.

In the following years, Mrs. Bloechl was my first grade teacher. Her room was on the opposite end of the same corridor as Kindergarten, right next to the stairway that lead to the second floor.

*Roosevelt School,
Grade 5, 1961-62*

Top Row: Rick (Fred) Auclair, Lily Fritz, Bobby Schock, Keith Kosmer, Bob Rockow, Wayne LaPoint, Paul Middlesteadt, Dennis Stuart
Second Row: Lana Zillges, David Schlichting, David Chapin, Jeff Walters, Edith Derr, Garret Galica
Third Row: Ellen Waite, Garry Moore, Mike Lichtenwald, Randy Domer, Nancy Rule, Sally Bartelt
Fourth Row: Mr. Frank Bremberger (Principal), Mrs. Amundson (Teacher), Tom Meyer, Steve Fenn
Bottom Row: Linda Schoeber, Cherie Clute, Kathy Hutchinson

Photo Credit: Randy Domer

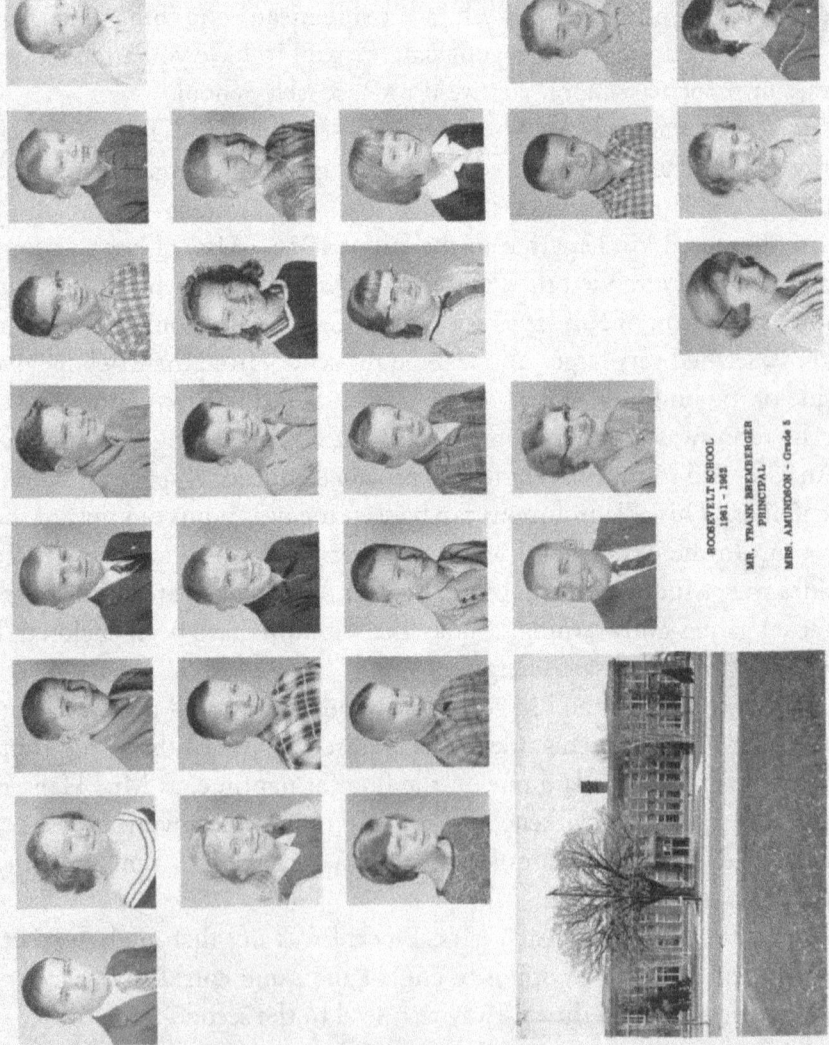

My second grade teacher was Mrs. Schroeder, third grade Mrs. Wagner, fourth grade Mrs. Fine, fifth grade Mrs. Amundson and sixth grade Mrs. Moenning. I liked all my teachers, but Mrs. Moenning was one of my favorites. Caroline Moenning had a personality that we all enjoyed. She had a wonderful sense of humor and would joke around with us. But when she needed to, she would get down to business and we knew the fun was over.

Mrs. Schroeder's Second Grade Class Roosevelt School 1958-59.

Back Row: Bobby Nicholson, Linda Schoeber, Ellen Waite, David Chapin, Lana Zillges, Edith Derr, Greg Hergert, Mike Langlitz, Dennis Stuart
Center Row: Bobby Schock, Ellie Weigandt, Roy Carpenter, Lily Fritz, Eddie Buttke, Phil Carpenter, Wayne LaPoint, Tom Merkel, Steve Koch
Front Row: Debbie Schuster, Cherie Clute, Randy Domer, Steve Jungwirth, Keith Kosmer, Terry Hoeft, Cherie Hartman, Phillip Hergert

Photo Credit: Randy Domer

In 1963 I entered Junior High School. Grades 7 through 9 were considered Junior High then. We had different teachers for different subjects. Mr. James Alderson was my home room teacher and also I had him for other subjects like geography, history and English. Mr. Lowell Johnson was our boys' gym teacher. A real disciplinarian, when he became irritated would purse his lips and look at you with his steely eyes. You wanted to crawl in a hole. I must say Mr. Johnson favored the more athletic kids during gym, so by now you can probably guess that didn't include me.

Other teachers included Mr. Joe Gerber (shop), Mr. Meikrantz and Miss Dahl (French), Mr. Novak (Math), Mrs. McDaniels (another of my favorites).

One of the Physical Ed teachers, Mr. Cutless, ran gym class like he was in Marine boot camp. If you did something wrong, you did laps or pushups, sometimes both. I remember one day he had the entire class doing pushups, and as he walked past me, he notice the chain around my neck bearing a Maltese cross had fallen out of the front of my shirt. Now, the Maltese cross meant nothing to me except I thought it looked cool, but the problem was they were not allowed to be worn in school. Not only did this infraction earn me some additional pushups, I was given detention. To make matters worse, I was then spotted wearing "Beatle Boots" which were black shoes with a higher heel and pointed toes, just like John, Paul, George and Ringo wore. Alas, they were also not allowed.

So here I am, after school, walking to "detention". If you don't know what detention is, its punishment handed out to bad boys and offenders…like me, I guess. I walked into the room, and there sat two of the "baddest" guys in our class. I won't mention names as they still may be around, and if they can read they may find a phone book and hunt me down. So here I was with a couple of "Fonzie" looking guys. I sat down in a desk a couple of seats away. They just stared at me, and my Maltese cross and Beatle Boots. I guess they couldn't believe I was here either. It was quite unnerving for me and needless to say, I ditched the Beatle Boots and tossed the Maltese cross, being careful not to draw any additional detentions the rest of my time in Junior High.

My classmates were all west siders until we entered junior high. It was then that many of the kids who lived in the country and went to elementary school near their home were bussed into to town. We called

Roosevelt School, c.1950
Photo Credit: Dan Radig, FB

them "farm kids" because, well, that's what many of them were. So, new friends were made and our class size grew.

It was during Junior High when I first remember taking an interest in girls. Some of us would have basement or garage dances at our house on Friday or Saturday night. The usual routine found all the boys on one side of the room, shy, goofing around, and maybe showing off a little for the girls. The girls would gather on the opposite side of the room and talk about, well, whatever it is that 13 year old girls talk about. Sometimes, the girls would dance with each other. It was usually late into the evening when the boys would finally muster enough courage to ask one of the girls to dance. It usually was your "girlfriend" or a girl you were hoping would become your girlfriend. Then when the last song was played (always a slow one), no one wanted the evening to end.

"Ebb Tide" and "You've Lost That Loving Feeling by the Righteous Brothers were big favorites. Bobby Vinton's "Mr. Lonely" or The Beach Boys "In My Room" would quickly bring the lights down.

About halfway through the party, the host's Mom would bring down pizza or a tray of BBQ sandwiches, chips and dip. The ceiling would be decorated with crepe paper and colored light bulbs replaced more traditional incandescent as they were too bright.

It was also during this time that "going steady" was popular. A boy would ask a girl to "go steady" and if she agreed, he gave her his ring. If the ring was too large for the girl's finger, she would wrap it with angora or mohair. "Going Steady" meant "hands off" to both sides. You didn't dare try to date a girl that was going steady with someone. Karen and I started "going steady" in high school on August 26, 1967, and eventually she agreed to marry me. She still has the ring I gave her too.

Not unlike most junior high schools in town, Roosevelt had a fight song. It was used at basketball and football games to motivate the team.

It was printed on the inside edge of our green and white book covers so it was easy to memorize. It went like this:

> "*Fight on, fight on for Roosevelt Junior High;*
> *that dear old green and white must always win;*
> *we have that spirit that is hard to beat;*
> *in all our games we never, never know defeat*
> *so come on boys and do your very best;*
> *and we will stay with you through every test;*
> *so we will sing and shout with*
> ***all*** *our might*
> *you're **dog gone** right*
> *for Roosevelt Junior High!*
> *U-rah-rah Rose-a-velt (clap)*
> *U-rah-rah Rose-a-velt (clap)*
> *Roosevelt…Roosevelt…Roosevelt! (Cheers)*

The gymnasium at Roosevelt School was something to behold. It was like no other in the city. The entire gym was about the same size as a regulation basketball court with about 12 inches to the walls around the sides. Students watched basketball games from the balcony as there was no floor space to seat fans. On the north end of the gym, a stage was used for school plays and the sort. That's where the Roosevelt Cheerleaders sat during gametime. During the time out, they would run onto the floor in their green and white outfits, and lead fans with a rousing rendition of the Roosevelt Fight Song, (which by now, I'm guessing, you can't get out of your head!). Visiting teams would make fun of our gym, some even calling it "a dungeon". But it was ours and we had so many great times there.

1967 was my sophomore year at Oshkosh High School. Oshkosh only had one public high school then, which is the building that is now Oshkosh West High School on Eagle Street. This was a big time in a kid's life as now you went to a school that included kids your age from all over the entire city. Our class size grew to over 600 students and although once you used to know every single person in your class, it was now too big to possibly know everyone.

One of my favorite memories in high school was 1968 when we won the state class A championship for football. Several of my high school pals played on that team. Fred Auclair was the biggest guy on the team and eventually played briefly for the Green Bay Packers during the NFL strike season of 1974. Friends Bill Fauk and Bill Zimmerman were standouts on the high school team as well.

In one of the pivotal games of this championship season, the Indians were facing their conference rival Fond du Lac in a late season contest at the Jackson Athletic Field. Fond du Lac was ranked #1 while Oshkosh sat in third in rankings. The OHS Indians need to win this game to have a chance for the championship. The Fondy team had an all state running back by the name of James Bond...that's right...shaken, not stirred. The Indian defense stiffened up that night, keeping Bond and his ground game in check well enough to keep the score close.

During the first half of the game, Fondy had the ball and was forced to punt. The punt returner for the Indians, Mike "Butch" Miller fumbled the ball and Fondy resumed possession deep in Indian territory on the 17 yard line. The Oshkosh defense stiffened, holding Bond to only 5 yards rushing in three downs. It was fourth down with the ball resting on the 12 yard line. Fondy sent the field goal team on to kick what would be the go ahead field goal and threaten OHS's chances for a championship. The crowd was worked into a frenzy. Indian Head Coach Harold Schumerth and Coach Fred Kubsch stood stoically on the sidelines, hoping this defense had enough gas left in the tank to stop this play.

It seemed like slow motion from this point on. The ball was snapped. It spiraled from the centers hands as the holder, arms extended, reached out to receive the ball. The ball went into his hands as he turned the seam side out and placed the ball on the spot...exactly where he wanted it. The Fondy kicker had already started his motion toward the ball. On his third step, his kicking leg went back and his foot connected with the ball as it started toward the uprights.

Suddenly from nowhere, around the end of the offensive formation, a blue and white jersey suddenly appeared. Number 34 flashed across the line and extended himself as far and long as he could. He felt the sting as the leather rebounded off his hands as the ball wobbled, flying off to the left, falling to the ground. The field goal was blocked! My buddy Mike Lichtenwald wore number 34 and it was this play that saved the game for the Indians. "Lichty" would be the first to tell you it was the effort of the entire team that won that game, and he is right. However, this is one memory he will cherish for a lifetime.

Final score…Oshkosh 13…Fond du Lac 6

In the final weeks of the season, Madison LaFollette moved up to the number 1 spot after Fondy's defeat, and then was unseated when they lost to Madison East, opening the door for the Indians to be State Champs.

The high school years were fantastically fun. By the end of our sophomore year, most classmates could drive. Cruisin' was a popular activity then. We would drive east on High Street to Main, then back to the west on Algoma Blvd. As they were both one way streets, they made the perfect "drag racing" strip. Main Street was also a great crusin' route since there were several pizza joints located there. Sandy's drive-in on Jackson between High and Algoma was a favorite spot. On the West Side, cars pulled in and out of Mars on Sawyer Street all night long.

On Friday nights, dances were the place to be. "Rec Dances" were held at the Recreation Gym on Division Street and "Park Dances" in the pavilion in South Park were the best. Live local bands would play and the dance floors were packed. "The Friends" was a local band that was a favorite with us as some of the members were fellow classmates. Tom Guenther was the drummer and the band has regrouped and performs around the area still today. "The Paul Bearers" featured southsiders Paul Muetzel (vocals) and John Prescott (drummer). On special occasions, like prom, Senior Girls or Senior Boys, we would import Milwaukee's godfather of soul… "Twistin' Harvey Scales and the Seven Sounds", a soul/show group.

Originally, the nickname was Oshkosh Indians. In 2002, the name was changed to the Wildcats due to sensitivity to Native Americans. (source: nativevillage.org)

The Class of '69 was special. Deep seated friendships made then are still strong today for many of us.

GO INDIANS!

Service Stations

Remember those days when gas was only nineteen cents a gallon? Two dollars worth of gas went along way in the 50's. And pump your own gas? Not back then.

Folks would pull their automobile into the station and roll across a black hose that was extended across both sides of the pumps. The hose was connected to a bell inside the station. Upon hearing the bell ring, an attendant would come bounding out the door. The attendant wore a uniform bearing the brand of gas they were buying, along with the attendant's name. The attendant's name in this story is Neil.

Neil came around the car to driver's window. "Fill 'er up!" or "Gimme two bucks worth", the driver would instruct him. Gasoline basically came in "Regular" or "Ethyl" then. Unless you specified Ethyl, the attendant assumed you wanted Regular.

Neil slid the metal hose nozzle into the gas tank, wound the handle on the side of the pump, which rolled the dollar amount on the pump dial back to zero, then began pumping the gas. While the tank was filling, Neil reached into his back pocket where he ALWAYS had a rag, and proceeded to wash the windshield.

Once the windows were washed, the hood was lifted. Neil reached in, grabbed the dip stick, checking to see if you needed to add any oil. Cars back then used oil and had to be "topped off" between oil changes.

If time allowed, Neil reached into his shirt pocket, grabbed a tire gauge and checked all four tires to ensure they were at the proper inflation per the tire manufacturer's specifications. If they were low, each station had air hoses right alongside the gas pumps. Each tire was inflated to the proper pressure, then Neil returned and removed the nozzle from the gas tank.

Finally, he returned to the driver's window and reported, "That'll be $4.20". The driver handed Neil a five dollar bill. Neil reached down in front of his belt to the coin changer that was connected, and clicked off eighty cents. He handed the change to the driver, then reached into his other shirt pocket and pulled out a book of S&H Green Stamps. Green Stamps were collected by patrons and could be redeemed for merchandise.

Then Neil would ask the driver to select an item from the glass enclosed premium display case between the pumps. Depending on how much gas you purchased you could select a roll of toilet paper, a juice size glass decorated with assorted fruit designs, colored glassware, stemware or other miscellaneous merchandise to reward you for your patronage.

I used "Neil" as my attendant to tell this story because my uncle Neil Ziebell owned a service station on the corner of 8th and Ohio Street, next door to Nigl's Bar and across the street from Punky's and Nigl's Bakery. Neil, and his business partner Herb Schneider, owned Schneider and Ziebell Standard Station.

In the 50's gas stations were known as *"filling stations"*. Unlike today's gas stations with mini marts that sell milk, bread, hot dogs, lottery tickets and beer, these businesses were true to their business. They sold fuel, oil and serviced cars. Schneider and Ziebell's Standard had two hoists and a car wash. You could get everything from an oil change and tire rotation to major things like engine repair, mufflers, brakes; things you would go to a "Service Dealer" for today.

There was no "lounge area" to wait for your car to be serviced. A couple of chairs were situated in the office area where customers could sit and wait for their car to be serviced if you didn't want to drop it off and come back. Hungry patrons could treat themselves to a small selection of candy bars in the vending machine or enjoy a handful of salted peanuts. They also gave away free road maps if you were planning to take a trip. Need new tires? They sold, mounted and balanced them while you wait.

The station was also a hangout for a number of guys that met there regularly throughout the day. The Guys consisted of a group of mixed backgrounds. Policemen, a DNR Warden, local stock car drivers, city employees and guys Neil and Herb knew showed up daily. They'd flip coins and the loser would buy sodas or walk across the street to Punky's and come back with a sack of burgers. With Nigl's Bakery right across the street, it was common to find a bag of donuts on the counter.

Just outside the door sat a Coke machine. Bottles of Coke, Jic Jac, Bireley's Orange and Goody Root Beer made up the usual assortment. Just insert your dime, select your "pop", grasp it by the top of the bottle and then slide it along the channels until it reaches the mechanism that released the glass bottle from confinement. As the bottle is lifted, the levers would allow the bottle to come free, and then lock again. In the front of the machine was a bottle cap opener mounted over a receptacle that caught the cap as it fell. A wooden pop case sat alongside the machine for empties.

Neil and Herb were both a bit entrepreneurial. In addition to the service business, they also rented trailers. Six or eight blue trailers of different sizes sat alongside the building and were available for rent.

My uncle Neil has been gone since 2004, but when I visit his cottage today, I'm reminded of those days when I open the cupboard and find the old juice glasses or walk into the garage and find a few old "oil rags" from the days when *filling stations* reigned supreme.

THE FAIRGROUNDS

I n the 1950's, the Winnebago County Fairgrounds stood proudly on the north edge of the city. The Fairgrounds operated on the property bordered by Murdock Ave to the south, Main Street to the east, Viola Ave to the north and Jackson Street to the west. It was the perfect location on what was then the outskirts of the city. This is where the city stopped and became rural. The property was spacious allowing for a very large grandstand overlooking a quarter mile dirt surface racetrack used for harness racing, stock cars and tractor pulls, several exhibition buildings and livestock housing for the county fair. Across the street on Murdock, Sno Cap, Leon's and The Hutch did big business, especially during fair time.

Kossel's Booth at the 1963 County Fair
Photo Credit: Dan Radig

The Fairgrounds wooden exhibition buildings were used to exhibit businesses like aluminum siding, home remodeling, flooring, cabinetry and more during the County Fair. Local businesses like Kossel's, Larry's TV and Appliance and Sears Roebuck were perennial occupants. Each retailer had a booth, proudly showing off their newest models of televisions, washer/dryers and refrigerators. And, if you purchased one at the fair, you earned the "fair discount".

Other buildings displayed award winning produce and home canned goods like jellies, preserves, fruits, vegetables, pickles…you name it! Local schools exhibited science projects and artwork from local students. It was always fun to go and see if any of the work you did in school were on display. Toward the north end of the property were the livestock areas. We never spent much time back there because of the odor and anyway, pigs, cows and sheep weren't really as interesting to us as getting the free yardstick from the home improvement area.

The largest building of all was the grandstand. The grandstand stood along Murdock Ave and took up more than half the block. The grandstand was used during the County Fair for spectators to watch the harness races and the spectacular entertainment acts. Performers like Bobby Vinton, The Three Stooges and countless other performers drew big crowds. One year, Myron Floren from the Lawrence Welk show performed with his accordion. As I was playing accordion and taking lessons from Sam Oswald at the time, I was interested and bought a ticket to the show. A girl I knew from school named

Ronnie Stopinski was invited to join Myron on stage and performed a song with him. Ronnie was very skilled with the accordion and what a thrill it was for me to watch someone I knew perform on stage with a big TV star! I can only imagine how thrilled she was. On August 30, 1960, Cowboy star Rex Allen performed the feature show while the *Harmonicats* entertained the audience with their comedy and music. In August of 1962, locals were treated to shows by Dennis Day and Jimmy Dean. The gate charge in 1962 was a mere 25 cents.

The Midway was operated by Steele's Amusements. As teenagers, we enjoyed taking our girlfriends to the fair and playing some of the games, in hopes of winning a stuffed animal. With odds so heavily favoring the house, as you would suspect, we always spent more than the prize was worth but had to keep trying until we won something. My favorite game to play as a kid was throwing the ping pong ball at a table of approximately 100 goldfish in bowls. The fish bowls each had one goldfish and the waters were colored with food coloring. That was pretty easy and we almost always went home with a goldfish. The midway featured rides like The Scrambler and Tilt-A-Whirl among many others to amuse kids and adults of all ages. The Merry-Go-Round and miniature cars were the favorites of the little ones. There was always a penny arcade, a tent that had games you could play for a penny, nickel or dime. These games were a little less technical than today's electronic offerings. Pinball machines were numerous and a movie machine that flipped black and white photos fast enough to give the impression you were watching an old movie. For a nickel, you could walk up to the booth where an animated plastic gypsy sat looking into her crystal ball. Once you put the coin in the slot, her arms began to move left and right and her head would nod up and down for about 10 seconds. Then a card would slide down the chute containing your fortune.

My favorite machine in the whole arcade though was a baseball card vending unit. For a nickel, you would get a large black and white card of a major leaguer. The display unit showed players like Willie Mays, Mickey Mantle and other big name stars. I plugged quite a few nickels in there trying to get one the super stars but usually came up with names like Moose Skowron and Jim Lemon. I still have the cards today, and have a difficult time finding their value as they are not very common. But their value to me is not their monetary worth. Each time I see the cards in my collection, I remember standing at that

THE FAIRGROUNDS

Southwest Entrance into the Fairgrounds
Photo Credit: Dan Radig

LEO'S SPEEDWAY IN OSHKOSH
PRESENTS THE
Winnebago County Fair Races
WEDNESDAY NIGHT
AUGUST 17, 8:15 P.M.
No Race, Tuesday, Aug. 16 — Due to Fair

LATE MODELS, SPORTSMAN AND STREET STOCK ELIMINATIONS
50-LAP FEATURE TROPHY RACE
FOR LATE MODEL STOCKS
$4,000 PURSE
TIME TRIALS 7:00   RACES 8:15

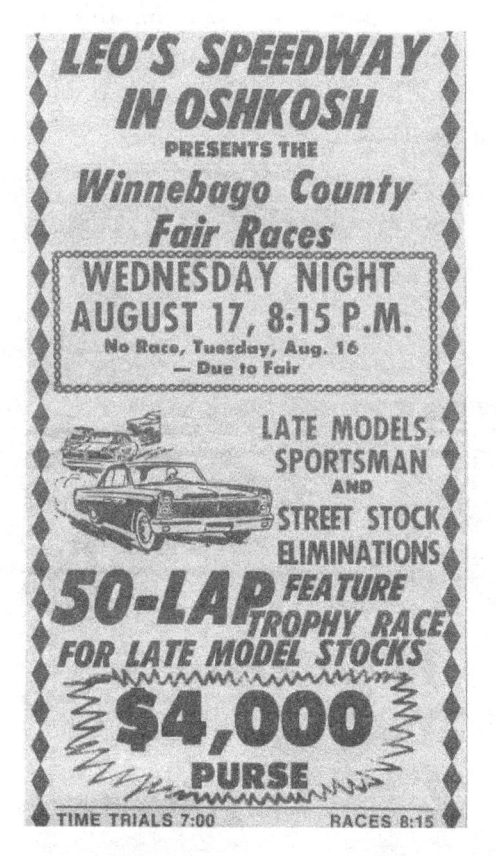

machine, spending my last few nickels with high hopes.

Along the Midway there were scattered beer stands. All four sides of the stand would be lined with men drinking their cold glass of *Chief Oshkosh* or *Peoples* beer, always the local favorite brands. A 8oz. glass of beer back then only cost a dime. Organizations like the Elks or Lions would have stands where they served food. Chicken, burgers, hot dogs and sweet corn were the main fare. Some local churches did the same and used the funds raised from the County Fair to support their programs.

Numerous concession stands were scattered about the entire fairgrounds offering cotton candy, pronto pups, sno-cones, taffy, peanuts, popcorn, caramel corn, pushups, drumsticks and all sorts of tempting treats.

The Winnebago County Fairgrounds was also home to another Oshkosh venue. Leo's Speedway offered fast action, stock car racing to fans from all over the Fox Valley. Stock car racing was big in the 50's and 60's and Wisconsin had some of the finest tracks and local drivers around. The Kaukauna and Slinger tracks were also part of the circuit. Wisconsin is a hotbed for producing great racers. Famous NASCAR drivers Matt Kenseth, Dick Trickle and Dave Marcus all put their early rubber down on Wisconsin tracks. And let's not forget the beautiful and talented Beloit native, Danica Patrick who is turning heads in both the NASCAR and Indy circuits today.

Tuesday night was race night at Leo's. Local drivers went head-to-head every week to earn points and win enough cash to keep their wheels turning. Leo's Speedway was a quarter mile dirt track located dead center in front of the grandstand.

I recall drivers like Lyle Diemel from Navarino, Jerry Smith from Medina, Bucky Wagner from Manitowoc, Clyde Schumacher and Glenn Bessette from Appleton, Claude Stadler from Oshkosh. And the very formidable George Giesen drove 7 JR.

Dave Conger and his #20 Outlaw
Photo Credit: Ed and August Tiedje

But Oshkosh native Dave Conger was the guy everyone tried be beat. Dave was one of the most popular drivers there. He drove the number 20 *Woody Woodpecker* car for several different sponsors over the years… Barney's Wrecker, Nubs and LeRoy's and West End Pizza to name a few.

Dave was a friend of my father's and part of the group that would hang out at Schneider and Ziebell's Standard filling station on 8th and Ohio Street. My dad was a part time sign painter and painted several of Conger's stock cars. It was my dad's idea to include Woody Woodpecker on all of Dave's cars. Driver Claude Stadler worked at the station as a mechanic, and Tuesday night, all the guys were at Leo's for the races.

The lineup each week would start with time trials. Each driver would come out and run two laps and his fastest time would determine where he started and in what heat. The slower drivers would compete in the first couple of heats, the faster ones in heats three and four. The feature race had the top finishers of each heat and sometimes would go as long as 50 laps!

George Giesen's 7 JR
Photo Credit: Bob Bergeron and dirtfan.com

Each race would put the fastest drivers in the rear of the pack at the start. It made for good exciting racing as those with the faster cars and better racing skills would weave through the pack to get to the front. Drivers who refused to "get out of the way" would find their rear bumper getting clipped, sending them into a spin as the potential leaders zipped on by toward the front.

Tempers would flare; fans would boo or cheer their favorite driver's fate. Each time there was an accident, the race would be re-started with cars in the position they were in at the time of the wreck. In the end, the winning driver was handed the checkered flag and did his victory lap, much to the elation or dismay of the fans.

A grandstand full of racing fans cheer as the race begins with the National Anthem
Photo Credit: Dan Radig, FB

During the race, vendors would carry cases of cold beer up and down the aisles. "Ice Cold Beeeeeer!" they would shout. Beneath the grandstand were makeshift bars were setup. Cold glasses of beer and soda were served there as well. The restrooms were located there as well, so between races, you could make a "pit stop", grab a beer and be back in your seat before the next race.

The speedway was operated by Leo Galica, the uncle to one of my best friends, Garret Galica. Garret and I went to many races starting at around age 9 or ten. My dad would take us and as Garret had "connections", we were free to wander about. Sometimes we even went into the "pit area" to watch the drivers work on their cars and get ready for the next race.

Admission was $1.15 for adults; children 60 cents and kids under 12 were free.

November 22, 1963

It was Friday, the last day of school for this week. The holiday season would soon be upon us and next week was Thanksgiving already. The excitement could be felt all around. Decorations filled the school's hallways and classrooms and we were all counting down the number of days left until we would soon all have time off from school.

Shortly after lunch, classes at Roosevelt School had just resumed when the school Principal came on the PA system. The announcement was both shocking and stunning, even for us seventh grade students. President John F. Kennedy had been shot in Dallas. Classes were being cancelled as all public schools were closing. Students were sent home until further notice.

When I arrived home, my mother was sitting in front of the television with tears in her eyes. President Kennedy was very popular with many Americans who embraced his youth and zest for family. I sat with her for some time, watching the news broadcast, trying to understand this horrible tragedy.

It was shortly past 1:30 pm central time when Walter Cronkite, who had been following and reporting the events, put on his black horned rim glasses, shuffled some papers, and announced to the country "From Dallas Texas, the flash, apparently official... President Kennedy died at 1pm central standard time...2 o'clock eastern standard time...some 38 minutes ago". Walter Cronkite was the most trusted reporter during this time and seeing him visibly shaken on network television helped me understand the gravity of what just happened.

Over the next few days, we continued to watch the coverage, not really understanding much of the political side of things, but knew it was terrible and we had a new President in Lyndon Baines Johnson.

The historic drama continued to unfold two days later on November 24th. We watched as accused assassin Lee Harvey Oswald was gunned down on live television by local Dallas nightclub owner Jack Ruby as Oswald was being transferred to another holding facility.

On the 25th of November, the nation mourned the loss of its young President. Television networks provided coverage of the President's body lying in State and funeral that followed. The image of young John Kennedy Jr. saluting his father's casket as it made its way to Arlington Cemetery is a memory we all still vividly have today.

During this time in our life, we were subjected to a number of tragic events such as this. The 60's were very turbulent times. The assassinations of Robert Kennedy and Martin Luther King, and the shooting of Presidential hopeful George Wallace, the building of the Berlin Wall to name a few, earmark the era of discontent over things like the Viet Nam War and uncertainty of the future of our country and world peace.

On the more positive side, we welcomed the Beatles, rock 'n rolled with Elvis, saw Neil Armstrong take the first step on the moon, celebrated Woodstock, visited Fantasyland with Walt Disney, met Barbie and Ken, sock hopped with Dick Clark and The American Bandstand, saw the introduction of color television and seat belts, played with hula hoops, watched in awe as Roger Maris surpassed Babe Ruth's single season home run record, witnessed Christiaan Barnard perform the first successful heart transplant, embraced the creation of the Polio Vaccine, cheered as the Green Bay Packers won the first Superbowl, saw Alaska and Hawaii become the 49th and 50th states, laughed with Red Skelton and much, much more.

Somehow, we made it through that difficult era of the 50's and 60's. In some ways I feel it made us stronger as a people and as a country, even though the pain and sense of loss sometimes felt overwhelming.

Perhaps you can remember where you were and what you were doing that fateful day on November 22, 1963 when you heard the news...

Acknowledgements and Credits

Many thanks to the following people who gave their time so generously and for sharing their wonderful memories and experiences

Karen Domer
Mrs. Jane Hutchinson
Kim Hutchinson Price
K Hutchinson
Jane Hutchinson Lichtenwald
James Senderhauf
August Tiedje
Ed Tiedje
Jay Ratchman
Andy Ratchman
Herb Tesch
Jean Zimmerman
Loretta Ziebell
Richard "Ticker" Reichenberger
Bill Gogolewski
Dan Radig
Peg Lautenschlager
Julie Krysiak Johnson
Jim Backus
Bill Wyman
Larry "Dutch" Rennert
Mara Munroe
Heather Rae Domer Connors
Winnebago County Historical and Archeological Society
Michael and Mary Strycker
Neil Knaggs
Jeff Weigandt
Steve Lawler

About The Author

Randy was born on July 29, 1951 to Donald and Geraldine (Ott) Domer. When Randy was about two years old, his dad built a home on Lark Street, a new residential area being developed on the west side of Oshkosh. The oldest of the three Domer kids, Randy attended elementary and junior high school at Roosevelt (Sawyer Street) and Oshkosh High School, graduating in 1969. In 1961, Stangel's opened a supermarket on N. Sawyer St., just south of The Club Tavern and across the street from the Sawyer Street Ball Park Ed Prescott purchased the store from the Stangel family in the mid 60's and hired Randy on his 15th birthday (a special work permit was required) as a carryout boy. Randy worked in this store at 313 N. Sawyer until 1985. Randy married Karen Steinert in 1970; they have 3 daughters and 6 grandchildren. He spent his early years as a meat cutter at Sawyer Street Supervalu. In 1986, Randy was hired by SUPERVALU, Inc. in Minneapolis where he worked in various corporate and regional office locations until 2009. Additionally, he was a member of the Wisconsin National Guard in the Oshkosh Unit, 1157 Transportation Company from 1968 to 1988.

Randy and his wife Karen have recently retired and moved back to their Oshkosh home on beautiful Lake Winnebago.

CPSIA information can be obtained
at www.ICGtesting.com
Printed in the USA
BVHW031718180120
569932BV00004B/529

9 781457 515880